Michael Ripper
Unmasked

Michael Ripper
Unmasked

by Derek Pykett

MIDNIGHT MARQUEE PRESS, INC.
Baltimore, Maryland

ISBN 1-887664-27-0
Library of Congress Catalog Card Number 99-63811
Manufactured in the United States of America
Printed by Kirby Lithographic Company, Arlington, VA
First Printing by Midnight Marquee Press, Inc., August 1999
Second Printing, October 2005

Acknowledgments: John Antosiewicz Photo Archives, Jim Coughlin, Tom Johnson, Jessica Miller, Mark A. Miller, John Stell, Linda J. Walter

For
Michael Ripper
A very special actor, gentleman and treasured friend

Table of Contents

Acknowledgments

Many people contributed to the production of this book by providing me with help, support, suggestions and invaluable information. All of which have made this long-overdue biography possible. They are:

Michael Ripper, who gave me permission and allowed me to write about his life and career.

Mum, Dad and my whole family to whom I shall always be eternally grateful, and without their continuous support nothing I have done would have been possible.

Luke Pykett, my younger brother, with his incredible typing and computer skills.

Christopher Lee, for taking time out of a busy schedule and writing me the Foreword.

Gary and Susan Svehla, my Publishers, for helping me to give Michael Ripper at least a bit of the recognition he deserves.

Andrew Thirlwall Potts, actor and friend, who first thought of the idea.

Brian Holland, a very dear friend and his wonderful family, whose endless kindness, support, help and encouragement has been nothing less than invaluable to me.

Danny R. Fulce and Michael and Karmellah Howlett, my very precious American friends whose help and support has also been invaluable.

Sandy Collis and Nick Wright, close friends who have helped me through the writing of this biography, and very patiently put up with my moaning when things were not quite going to plan.

Ian Tyler, whose treasured friendship, sense of humor and help I can always rely on.

Martin Killeen for his wonderful friendship, for listening and finally for being so interested in my work.

John Stell for being so kind and writing a chapter for this biography.

Cecelia Doidge-Ripper, Susan Peters, Peter Ripper, Norman Mitchell, Bruce Montague, Jean Anderson, Peter Copley, James Ellis, Alan Curtis, Bill Owen, Brook Williams, Eddie Powell, Michael Gough, Jenny Laird, John Thaw, Lionel Jeffries, Geoffrey Bayldon, Ronnie Barker, Martin Benson, Peggy Mount, Maurice Denham, Sir John Gielgud, Jill Kelly, John Looby, Brenda Marshall, Paul Pickford, Jonathan Brooks, Thomas Laxton, James Keeble, Peter Siddon and Melanie Edington, Frank J. Dello Stritto, Kathy Higgins, Willoughby Gullachsen, Elmar Podlasky, Donald Fearney, Jane Clark, George Burke, Tiffany Parish and Larry Allen of Amazing Space and Gainsborough Film Studios, Margaret McCully of the Central School of Speech and Drama, David Smith of Castaside, Melanie Trifona Christoudia and Janet Birkett of the Theatre Museum, Ian O'Sullivan and Richard Hogg of the British Film Institute, Andre and Lisa Barry of Fotostop Express, Hammer Film Productions, L'Epine Smith & Carney, Kobal Collection, Theatre Despatch, BBC's Written Archive Centre, British Actors' Equity Association, Portsmouth Grammar School, BBC Television, Anglia Television, Granada Television, Thames Television, Yorkshire Television.

All of whom I couldn't have done this without. To all of the above a big thank you, and I shall always be forever grateful.

Photographs Courtesy of: Michael Ripper, Cecelia Doidge-Ripper, Susan Peters, Peter Ripper, Sandy Collis, Willoughby Gullachsen, Jim Coughlin, Tom Johnson, Mark A. Miller
Playbills Courtesy of: David Smith (Castaside)
Caricatures Courtesy of: Paul Pickford, Susan Peters

Michael Ripper

Foreword

When the Australians use the word "ripper," it signifies approval and is used as a term of endearment.

When I use it, I do so with a capital R and preface it with the name "Michael." My feelings parallel those of the Australians.

During my travels around the world, whenever the name Hammer comes up—which it does quite frequently, people invariably say to me "Oh yes, we much enjoyed this or that film: But then of course Michael Ripper was in it, which made it unforgettable." My own contributions are appreciated, but they pale in comparison.

Michael, to me and to many others, represented all that is best in our profession in his many varied and memorable performances. Dedication, total involvement and complete professionalism: qualities not all that much evident today. He was equally adept in major or lesser roles and always created fully formed characters, which never failed to make an impression. He was brilliant in comedy—his drunken poacher in *The Mummy* is unforgettable. He always made a very good "heavy." Was it first or second murderer in the film *Richard III* or perhaps both together?

I always felt I was playing a supporting part in a Michael Ripper production—and was happy to do so. When he said in *The Pirates of Blood River*, "I'm on your side Cap'n," I became deeply suspicious and rightly so. He is the only actor who consistently made me laugh uncontrollably and he knew it. In spite of his cherubic appearance, he is really a friend at heart. He is one of the imperishable contributors to British and international cinema. Long may he be with us.

Christopher Lee
London 1998

Introduction

When I was younger, long before I was a friend of Michael Ripper's, I used to turn on the television just to watch him in films. Whether it be one of the St. Trinian's films or a Hammer Film. I can remember watching *Captain Boycott, Oliver Twist* and even a *P.C. 49* film because I knew Michael Ripper would be making an appearance.

Today, I feel I am a close friend of Michael's and whenever I meet up with him it's always an enormous pleasure. I always shake hands and greet him by saying, "How are you Michael?" and he always responds, "Well, I'm still alive."

Each time I am with Michael, especially when watching some of his film work with him, I think to myself, is it really him? Is it really the Michael Ripper who's appeared in over 100 movies (quite an achievement for one actor), shaken hands with, and stood alongside many famous British and American stars—many of whom are mentioned in the pages of this biography?

Michael is a quiet man, soft spoken and extremely modest. He takes great delight in meeting people. Upon meeting my family for the first time, he greeted them with the same warmth and kindness with which he has always greeted me.

When I first asked Michael if I could write a biography about his life and career, he said, "Do you really think it will sell?" It is very sad that an actor like Michael should think such a thing. He is an actor adored by many people, including myself. He is also highly respected by his fellow professionals.

When visiting with Michael rarely has the actor in him raised his head. However, I do once remember as he helped me into my coat he jested, "Your coat, Sir." I swear Michael delivered a similar line playing Louis the manservant in the film *The Story of Gilbert and Sullivan*. It was a treasured moment for me as the line was delivered with the unmistakable Ripper timing.

I have no doubt, that if Michael were still working today as a character actor, he could hold his own with today's brightest actors (even though Michael sadly thinks otherwise). I honestly believe you never lose the talent you've been given.

Since I began writing this biography, the response from Michael's fellow colleagues has been excellent. Not once have these wonderful people not wanted to help in the best way they can, and I have only been greeted with kindness and support. Michael's name seems to bring out the best in people; he is universally loved and respected by his fellow professionals.

I would like to mention Michael's friend Norman Mitchell, who, every time I phoned for help, made me laugh uncontrollably with stories about Michael and his own career in show business. Norman is a true comic and fabulous storyteller.

Recently it was an absolute pleasure for me to escort Michael to see his old friend Jean Anderson at her home in Kensington, London. They hadn't seen each other in over 50 years, but when they met, it seemed as though no time had passed. It was a sheer delight to be there and witness this wonderful reunion.

Also, I was very lucky and privileged to be able to escort Michael to a Hammer Films reunion at Bray Studios.

Even more recently, I arranged (with a bit of help from my actor friend, Andrew Thirlwall Potts) to take Michael around the old Gainsborough Film Studios where he had appeared in several classic British movies. We were chauffeured in a comfortable Mercedes to the studio by a very lovely lady, Jane Clark, and then shown around the studio by a very kind gentleman, George Burke, who used to be a scene shifter there in the 1930s. The studio itself closed many years ago, but the empty, desolate building still stands.

It was a poignant and ghostly trip down memory lane for Michael. The building echoed with chatter and haunting laughter of many a famous name that graced the studio floor in its heyday. The eerie atmosphere conjured up many images. You could almost see the ghostly figures of Stewart Granger, James Mason and Alastair Sim vacating their dressing rooms and striding along the endless corridors. It was a cherished experience for both me and Michael, and with the help of my close friend and photographer, Sandy Collis, we managed to capture some pictures of Michael roaming around the place.

Sadly, the inside of Gainsborough Film Studios is now being renovated, and only the outside of the building will remain as it was. It is nice to think that we actually got to see the inside of the studio for the last time while it looked exactly the same as when Michael worked there. Also, George Burke gave us a souvenir to remember our visit to Gainsborough. It was the last remaining piece of scenery left at the studio: a black wooden side view head cutout of Alfred Hitchcock. This late, great master of filmmaking made two of his films at Gainsborough—*The Lodger* and *The Lady Vanishes*. Michael was actually filming at the Gainsborough in 1938 when Hitchcock was making the latter of the two films, but unfortunately, Michael cannot recollect ever meeting the famous director.

With this homage I hope to prove to Michael and remind his many fans what a very special person Michael Ripper is, and that he is remembered and beloved much more than he could ever imagine. I, for one, am proud and honored to be his friend.

Michael and his wife, Cecelia, have been marvelous to me since I first met them both. To be in their company is always fun and an enormous pleasure.

Cecelia is a lovely lady, has been a great help to me, and like many others has put up with my almost constant pestering since I first started writing this biography. I am sure that on more than one occasion she probably wanted to tell me to bugger off, but because of the charming person she is, she would only think of helping me and very kindly thanking me for being so kind to Michael.

In many ways I wrote this biography to pay Michael back for all the glorious days I have been lucky enough to spend in his company. But I feel that he truly deserves this dedication to his life and career and it should really have been written a long time ago. However, in a way I must thank God it wasn't, and that I was finally given the enormous privilege of being able to write it for him. This book for Michael will be a highlight of my life.

Finally, Michael has been like a grandfather to me, and he has treated me very much like a son. All I can hope for now is that I can spend many more days and years in the company of this true gentleman.

God Bless you Michael and thank you for being my friend. I shall never ever forget you or the kindness you have shown towards me.

Derek Pykett
July 1999

Hollywood

In early 1950 a young Michael Ripper was called to the offices of Coronado Productions, Wigmore Street, London. He was set to audition for the part of Sam Baxter in David E. Rose's film *Your Witness*.

The role he was reading for was his first as a lead—all of Michael's film work up till then had always been as supporting character. Michael entered the office and was introduced to the director of the film, Hollywood actor Robert Montgomery, who would also be playing a role in the movie. Montgomery liked Michael immediately. The first initial reading was a great success. However, Montgomery wished to see more of Michael's work. He asked to view Michael's performance as Pat Nolan in *Captain Boycott*, a film which was produced by General Films in 1947 starring Stewart Granger. Michael had a praiseworthy supporting role. Upon seeing the film, Montgomery would make his final decision as to whether Michael would be cast in the lead. A week later Montgomery delivered the line that made Michael Ripper happier than any other he can remember during his career in show business, "You work on Monday."

An exciting time indeed. Michael was to play a leading role in a Hollywood film (even though it was to be made in England). This was the film which could lift his career and thrust him into international stardom.

After the film was completed, Robert Montgomery, as he was making his way back to America, was interviewed by a local reporter at Shannon Airport. Montgomery said:

> Michael Ripper is a really fine actor and I can see a great screen career in store for him. A series of pictures is now planned, all starring this very versatile young man.

Michael thought his career would be on the upswing, although, sadly it was not to be. The film turned out to be a box-office flop and the series of pictures Montgomery had promised fell through.

Michael Ripper relaxing on the set of *Your Witness* (Warner Bros., 1950).

However, Montgomery did offer Michael a chance to go to Hollywood, where he said "Good screen work would be waiting." Michael decided to turn the offer down and stay with the English film industry. He decided the Hollywood star treatment was not for him. It would be the first and last time a proper offer like this would be made, and *Your*

Studio portrait from *Your Witness*

Witness would be the only time Michael would be cast as the lead in a film.

Where would he have been if he had taken up that Hollywood offer and how different would his career have been?

In many ways let us be thankful that he stayed behind, for Michael Ripper will leave us a legacy of great supporting performances in both film and television, especially in the classic Hammer films. Michael was not a leading man, but rather a great character player, and he felt that his best work would only occur on English soil. He was right.

An Unhappy Childhood

Michael George Ripper, son of Harold and Edith Ripper, was born in Portsmouth, England on January 27, 1913.

As a baby Michael suffered from diphtheria and spent much of his time in and out of hospitals. Michael's own first personal memory goes back to the age of two.

He was sitting in the kitchen in a basket chair. His mother, Edith, was preparing the evening meal when his father returned after a busy day at Portsmouth dockyard where he was employed as a civil servant. For no reason at all (as far as Michael remembers) Harold said to Edith while pointing at little Michael, "This boy's becoming a real mother's boy, I'm going to take him in hand." He then thrashed Michael across the face knocking the two-year-old from the basket chair to the floor. For the next few years Michael would live in fear of his father's untimely thrashings which would include being beaten with a heavy wooden cane. Each beating left the child frightened and bruised. His mother, sadly, would do nothing to stop this abuse—she probably lived in fear of Harold and dared not to speak up in defense of her son. What hurt Michael the most was the fact that there was no real reason for the beatings he suffered. He cannot remember being a badly behaved child, so why did his father respond this way?

Michael's feels that perhaps his father suffered the same fate at the hands of his own father when he was young. Michael does remember that on occasion his father did show him affection, but he also loved taking the cane to him. I am sure for a young boy this abuse must have been quite frightening and confusing.

Fathers of that era were quite strict and punishment was swift and commonplace and often for the smallest of offenses. Though with each caning Michael would become stronger and stronger, and he eventually learned to deal bravely with each new beating.

Harold Ripper once said he considered his son Michael something of a problem child, but all Michael can remember is being a quiet little boy who very rarely stepped out of line. As a youngster Michael would

Michael Ripper at age two in 1915.

take walks along Portsmouth dockyard and watch the huge ships and hundreds of navy men who were stationed there. He also enjoyed very much going on bicycle rides with his younger brother Peter, who was born in 1916. The Ripper family lived at 18 Allambra Road, Southsea and also included Barbara, a sister to whom Michael was very close.

Michael's school days were mostly spent at Portsmouth Grammar school where his loving brother Peter was also a pupil. Those school years were something of a disaster. Michael was not a gifted pupil and began to hate each and every day he spent in the confines of the   school.

However, he did shine in one subject — history. He loved to answer all the questions that the teacher asked, never letting any of the other pupils get a word in edge-wise. The young Michael was always jumping from his seat, raising his hand and shouting "SIR!" One day the teacher (whom Michael remembers as a friendly man) lost his temper and said, "Oh, Ripper, go outside." It wasn't an unkind gesture towards the young Michael, but the poor teacher only wanted other children to be able to answer some of the questions. In the long corridor outside the classroom

A family photograph: (From left to right) Michael's younger brother Peter, his mother Edith, Michael and his father Harold. (1918)

he waited, not quite understanding what he was supposed to have done wrong.

While waiting, the headmaster Reverend W.J. Barton (whom all the pupils hated and were really quite frightened of) approached. "What are you doing here Ripper?" he asked in a deep voice. A nervous young Ripper replied, "The teacher told me to go outside, Reverend Sir." So in his next breath and in an even deeper voice the headmaster said, "Very well, go to my study." Michael instantly knew his fate and walked slowly towards the study door with Barton walking behind. Pushing the door open Michael followed the headmaster into the infamous study where many a naughty student had been given a good caning—but Michael had done nothing wrong. Barton told Michael to bend over the back of the chair; his fate was obvious. The Reverend lifted his cane from its black box and proceeded to give Michael six heavy strokes across his lower back. The pain was severe, but Michael left the office without shed-ding a tear—he had unfortunately become used to this type of caning.

On his return home his mother noticed her son was holding his lower back and looked distraught when he told her what had happened. She lifted his shirt and what she saw was nothing less than diabolical; the bruises across his lower back were long and enormous. Furious, Michael's mother (who was a teacher herself at Drayton Road School, Portsmouth) took her son's hand, left the house and headed straight for Portsmouth Grammar School to confront the man responsible for this brutal attack on her son. However the Reverend W.J. Barton was not one of the easiest men to challenge. Though he could be suave, eloquent and persuasive, there was a certain arrogance about him which made people uncomfortable in his presence. He seemed to deliberately seek this effect. However, this type of arrogance would not work with Michael's mother. Edith told him that she would take court action against him. But Michael was not in favor of this, so Reverend W.J. Barton was let off the hook.

At school Michael did have many friends, most of whom were prefects and a good deal older than himself; these older friends would look after him during the school day and made sure nobody gave him a difficult time.

In fact, he spent as much time as he could with them even out of school — he was only too happy to get away from his home and dominant father.

At school Michael would take part in many of the school plays, often playing very good roles. Once again this was due to his father, who pushed him into this sort of thing.

Harold Ripper, in his spare time, was an amateur dramatic producer and ran several drama groups. He was also an elocutionist and taught people to speak poetry. As a speech therapist he would teach Michael how to enunciate clearly, and the young Michael would be forced to enter several competitions for recitation.

Michael was not happy about this; in fact, he was an unhappy child and being forced to do things that he wasn't quite sure he really wanted to do did not make the situation easier. It wasn't that he didn't enjoy drama or even reading poetry, but it was because his father was so assertive with him and most certainly did not make it easy for the young boy.

Harold Ripper was a very well-spoken man, about six feet tall, slim, with a very serious face. Edith Ripper was quite a beautiful looking lady, with short black wavy hair. A lady who most certainly knew who was the ruler of the house.

On the beach at Hayling Island in 1925 are (from left to right) Michael, Barbara, Edith and Alastair Sim.

The Rippers were not a particularly well-off family, but the house where they lived was always clean and well kept and Michael and his brother and sister were always very well clothed. However, Michael was so unhappy his health began to suffer as a result.

Apart from Michael's father who was interested in theatre and liked to practice its teachings, no other member of the Ripper family was theatrically inclined.

Michael, even at his very young age, was well on his way to becoming the first professional theatrical member of his family, and his father went to great lengths to ensure that his son stayed on this path. He most certainly wanted his son to have this as a future career. Michael was unsure what he really wanted to do with his life but unable to override the will of his father, he became an actor. His mother was also in favor of her son going into the acting field. Whenever they could, his parents entered Michael

In the garden at Southsea in 1925 are (from left to right) Barbara, Alastair Sim and Harold Ripper. Michael is standing behind Sim.

into poetry-reciting competitions. One of these was the Oxford Verse speaking competition. It was here that Harold Ripper became friendly with a gentleman who would become a close friend of the family. The man in question would also become one of England's greatest comedy character actors, Alastair Sim, whose performance as Scrooge in 1954's *A Christmas Carol* would gain him worldwide fame.

When Michael finally made it into the acting profession, Sim's name would turn up on several occasions. They never became close friends; it was only a working relationship. Michael seems to think his father may have had something to do with this; perhaps Harold Ripper had told Alastair to keep his distance from his son.

Harold and Alastair were close friends and Alastair was a regular visitor to the Ripper household in Southsea. Many of the discussions centered around drama and poetry. After listening to many of these conversations, Michael would soon start to take a keen interest in the theatrical world and often would visit the theatre or cinema.

"God bless us, every one!"

These Wonderful Words
Have Warmed the Hearts
of Millions the World Over

"Christmas? Bah! Humbug"

A new
Screen
Triumph!

"a Christmas Carol"

"I'm sure we shall
none of us forget
Tiny Tim!"

"Christmas has done me good...
and will do me good... and
I say, God Bless It!"

ALASTAIR SIM · · · CHARLES DICKENS "A CHRISTMAS CAROL"

Was this really the career he wanted? He began to think it was. Could it be an escape for him from his unhappiness? He was 14 and desperately wanted to get away from his home and school. Could acting be his ticket to a new and different life? This was when young Michael began to become an actor as he tried to please his demanding father.

Michael's depression was beginning to become quite noticeable. When he was 14, an enlightened doctor gave him his liberty and he left school a happier child, but there was still one more escape to make. He told Harold he definitely wanted to become an actor, which he knew would please his father.

It was here that Harold got together with Alastair Sim to talk about his son's future. The two men were a perfect match, both very reserved although Alastair was a much friendlier man than Harold.

His father, according to Michael, was cool; his mother Edith, on the other hand, could have a great sense of humor and be very witty. Unfortunately, when her husband was around this humor didn't often surface. She would always listen to Harold and never speak out against him, even if she knew he was wrong.

Alastair Sim did bring a different atmosphere to the Ripper household. When he was visiting the tension that was nearly always in the air (especially between Michael and his father) would often drop, and Harold became a changed man just for the few hours that Alastair was in his company. The family would also have many happy outings with Sim. On many occasions they would visit Hayling Island just off the coast of Portsmouth.

Michael's future was eventually decided. Acting it would be. It was decided he would audition at the Central School of Speech and Drama in London. In the audition Michael read a poem, which his father had helped him rehearse. The young Ripper was instantly given a place, a scholarship was awarded, and Michael was to join the course in October 1928. Finally at age 15 he escaped from the life and home where he was so unhappy.

His new address would be 325 Upper Richmond Road, Putney, in the southwest of London. This would most certainly be a new start in his life — Michael would grow apart from his family, a family which had never really been close. They would meet, but it would never be the same again. Michael was to become a self-sufficient actor.

His relationship with his father would never improve, and Michael would always resent the punishments given when he was younger. To this very day Michael cannot forgive his father. He does however remember his mother with love and affection, and he can forgive her, even if she did not step in when she should have. Edith Ripper died in 1966.

It was just after her death that Michael received a phone call from his father. Harold said, "Come down to Portsmouth son, and take me back to our old house." Perhaps Harold was finally trying to make up with his son. However, Michael did not accept his father's invitation. In fact, he became as unpleasant as his father had been to him. Michael's only response was "No way." They would never talk or meet again. Harold Ripper died in 1967.

Michael did attend his father's funeral. Whatever happened between father and son was hopefully, not all bad. In fact, we should be thankful to Harold Ripper for spotting his son's talent and giving him the chance of an acting career. And for giving audiences a chance to see Michael Ripper enact classic performances on stage and television and in films.

The Young Actor

The Central School of Speech and Drama was based at the Albert Hall, Kensington, in London when Michael attended. His days at the school were enjoyable even though he admits they were rather strict — but nobody would ever lift a cane to him — a fact he was most pleased to learn.

He was thought to be a highly gifted and talented drama student by his tutors. It was most certainly a great learning experience for the young Ripper and he used the knowledge he gained to its full extent.

The studying at Central included theatrical history and the art of speaking clearly. Michael had become something of an expert in elocution since his father was a speech therapist. Other lessons included improvisation, breathing exercises, reading plays — from Shakespeare to the Restoration period, enacting many different kinds of roles — old, young, comedic, serious — and the art of applying greasepaint. Michael would also learn the acting techniques of Brecht and Stanislavsky.

Many an evening he would take his work back to his hotel accommodation on Upper Richmond Street, and go through his paces. When he did get time off and could afford it he enjoyed shopping on Kensington High Street. Shopping for clothes was a particularly favorite pastime.

Another important part of his life then were various young ladies. Michael admits that even though he was only 15, one or two young girls did slip in and out of his life during his stay at the Central School.

After a year at the Central School, a year which turned out to be more difficult than he originally thought, he was finally ready to leave. He would depart with an assortment of new skills under his belt, including singing and dancing. He later said, "I was never a good singer, but could dance a little." In July 1929 he left the Central School and was now ready to find his first acting engagement.

Michael needed a good agent. He would finally sign with Peter Eade who was located at 28 Cork Street, London. Eade immediately sent him to the Grand Theatre, Fulham in London. It was here Michael joined his first repertory company and played his first part as the juvenile in *The Ringer*. It was his first professional job and he remembers it as being extremely difficult.

In repertory you had to learn your part quickly and keep up with the brisk pace. This was the true training ground for any would-be actor. Most of the things Michael learned at the Central School had to be thrown out of the window. Michael later said:

Grand Theatre, Fulham

> You didn't really have time to think about the part, you
> just had to go on and do it.

Stage nerves were strung tight worrying about any would-be disasters that could happen during a live performance. Michael was only 16, so it was especially tough for him. Actors would regularly forget lines, and trying to ad-lib under such pressure was not easy. Props would sometimes not be in their place and often doors wouldn't open on the stage backdrops. Michael had to be ready for all of these disasters, and of course, he was a victim of inexperience.

After *The Ringer* Michael's next production at the theatre was *Belladonna.* In the second act of this production he had three entrances. However, on the night of the first performance, Michael, by now settled into his dressing room listening to Philadelphia Orchestra records, missed his first entrance in the second act altogether. The poor actors on stage had to ad-lib his lines since his dialogue was extremely important to the play's plot. Realizing he had missed his cue, he rushed onstage and delivered the same lines all over again. The director was furious and Michael got his first reprimand — most of which is unrepeatable in polite company. In fact, he was nearly sacked, which would not have been good since had only been out of drama school for a few weeks.

He was eventually rescued from the terrible embarrassment of his exploit by a speech training pupil of his father's, Arthur Brough. He offered Michael another job in repertory, in Folkstone, Kent, where Brough was running a company. Michael was far more successful here, and at the tender age of 17 earned £6 a week, which in the slump of 1930 was quite an achievement.

Portrait from 1930

Brough was very pleased with the young Ripper's work, and Michael followed Folkstone with a tour in which he understudied Emlyn Williams in George Bernard Shaw's play *Misalliance*. Michael would wait anxiously, hoping that Williams would fall ill or take a day off. But Emlyn never missed a performance due to illness, he was a true professional. However, he did give Michael a couple of opportunities to sub for him.

After the tour finished, Michael worked for a short time at the Old Court Theatre, Sloane Square, in London. During a brief time off from his labors at the Old Court, he decided to return home to Southsea for a few days... a trip which turned out to be his undoing.

He gave an interview to the *Portsmouth Evening News* about being an actor and working at the Old Court. During this interview he lied, giving his age as 23. The newspaper checked the facts, and printed his true age of 17. The Old Court Theatre somehow found out about this and Michael got fired—the excuse being irresponsibility.

After his untimely firing from the Old Court, Michael heard about dancing classes taking place in Southsea, and decided, since he was out of practice, to check them out. The classes were run by a gorgeous young woman called Jean Bramley. Michael fell instantly in love with her, and after a few weeks they started dating. Eventually they went ballroom dancing together. Their relationship was sealed and Jean would soon become Michael's wife. The relationship did not however come without its problems.

Even after the sacking Michael's foot was soon back in the stage door, and before long he had joined a touring theatre company, which was run by Anew MacMaster. The entire company soon set sail for Ireland. In the company was another young actor named Reginald Knowles; later this young man would change his name and become screen star Patric Knowles, famous for his work in films, including Universal's *The Wolf Man*.

When the slump hit show business in 1931 and theatres began to close, Michael found himself once again back in repertory with Arthur Brough at Folkstone. When this theatre closed, another friend of Michael's father's came to his aid. This time it was not an acting job, but the job of projectionist at the Apollo, a new super cinema that had just opened in Southsea.

Michael was 18 and admitted this job was the most soul-destroying part of his life. He said, "You just stood by a machine waiting for something to go wrong." Most of his time, when not working at the cinema, was spent with Jean. It was during 1931 that they decided to get engaged. Jean was 18. However, her parents did not approve of Michael, and Jean's mother would not give her daughter consent to marry until she

Michael Ripper and his first wife Jean Bramley at Bexhill in East Sussex, 1934.

was 21—three years away. No matter, they stayed together despite the slight problems and finally got married on March 3, 1934. The marriage ceremony was a small gathering at a registry office.

Michael was eventually saved from the operator's box at the cinema, and was soon back in the acting saddle. He joined the Bexhill Repertory Theatre in East Sussex, and for a whole year he played leading parts in a twice weekly change of program.

However daunting the early cinema experience might have been, it was still a job— Michael needed money to look after himself and Jean. So despite the strenuous schedule of plays and rehearsals, he went to work at the cinema three times a week.

Michael says his career took off in 1935 when he joined the Festival Theatre in Cambridge.

From here he went with a group of actors to the Theatre Royal, Rochdale, in Greater Manchester. Each and every play they performed fell flat on its face before the unyielding audience. So in desperation they turned to *Sweeney Todd.* Michael said:

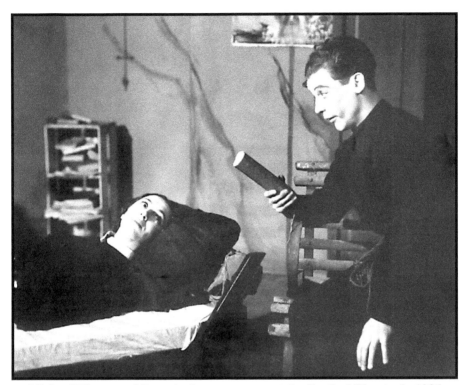

Michael Ripper and Jean Anderson onstage at the Festival Theatre in 1936.

> It was dreadful, but for some reason it packed them in. It ran for an incredible three months.

After this Michael returned to London, and a chance meeting with Alastair Sim led to an introduction to George Smith, who ran a film studio at Walton-on-Thames just outside London. At the age of 22, Michael's career in films would finally begin.

His first role, a very brief one, was with James Mason and Robert Rendel in the film *Twice Branded*. Mason plays the snobbish and unforgiving son of an ex-convict who returns from jail to try ro rebuild a family life. The film was directed by Maclean Rogers, who would go on to direct several early films featuring Michael. The two of them would become good friends, and Michael later said, "Maclean Rogers was the man that introduced me to British cinema." James Mason was quite young and also a newcomer to films. Mason was rather stagy in these early movies, as were many actors who had a strong theatre background. They had to learn a new acting technique to accommodate the silver screen. Michael remembers that Mason, even at this very young

Margaret Inchbold and Michael Ripper perform at the Festival Theatre in Cambridge in 1936. Despite the make-up he was only 23 at the time.

age, was a deeply private man, always appearing somewhat troubled, and desperately trying to learn his new craft.

Michael's second film, *Prison Breaker*, would also be with the young Mason and under the direction of Adrien Brunel. Michael watched Mason's technique grow from scene to scene—his velvet voice was beginning to shine through even then.

During a break in making these quickie films, Michael had time to return to the Festival Theatre, Cambridge. It was here that he met Jean Anderson, who was married to Peter Powell. These two would play a big part in Michael's theatrical career for the next 11 years.

Peter Cross, David Raven, Jean Anderson and Michael Ripper onstage in 1936 at the Festival Theatre in Cambridge.

In 1936 Powell started his own theatrical company, The Seagull Player's, at the Little Theatre in Leeds. From Cambridge Michael went with Jean Anderson to Leeds to join her husband. It was here that Powell gave Michael the chance to play Shakespeare as well as to act in the best modern plays. Also in this company was a young actor called Peter Copley, who three years later would join Michael, Jean Anderson and Peter Powell at the Gate Theatre in Ireland.

Productions moved along smoothly at the theatre. However, they were not without their incidents. During rehearsals for one play, the actors rehearsed in a rather run-down room and once found themselves face to face with a deadly situation. At first they didn't realize anything was wrong. The night before the rehearsal in question, the actors had been out partying, and all of them, including Michael, had drunk well over the limit. So the next day in rehearsal none were in the best of shape. Problems started when Jean Anderson, playing the leading lady, watched her colleagues collapse one by one. Each dropped down like a lead weight. One actor, then another, and then Michael, and they all thought that drink was the problem or perhaps food poisoning. Jean Anderson recalled, "It was quite frightening to watch them all drop, and almost carried from the room." Things got worse when Anderson herself collapsed. "It was an awful feeling," Anderson recalled. "You could just not keep on your feet. The worst thing of all is that we had a performance that evening, which I had to do in the end mostly sitting down." All the actors recovered, but the cause wasn't what they expected. In the corner of the room that they had used for rehearsals was an old stove that had been   releasing dangerous fumes which overcame the actors.

The play they had been rehearsing was none other than *Macbeth*, a production which has often seen its fair share of difficulties and

Robert Hobbs, Norman Pierce, Michael Ripper and Gus McNaughton in *Busman's Holiday* (RKO, 1936).

on many occasions seems to have been cursed.

While in Leeds Michael stayed in a hotel with his wife Jean, who was now heavily pregnant with their first and only child. When Jean realized it was getting close to the time to deliver the baby, she returned home to Southsea and left Michael in Leeds to continue his work in the plays.

One night after the actors had finished their performance they heard that Lord Reith had told the country that the King of England's life was drawing quietly to its close, or whatever the now-disputed wording was. The

As Crook in *Busman's Holiday* (**RKO, 1936**).

shutdown of the theatres following King George V's death meant that Michael would have to part company with Jean Anderson and Peter Powell, and sadly leave the Seagull Players behind. Michael would have fond memories of this company which had given him his first proper chance to play meaty roles.

Michael returned to London, determined to seek his future there. His first job on his return to the capital was a part in a play at the Arts Theatre. Michael played the character of Enoch Bryant in a play called *Little Ol' Boy*. In the same company was Esmond Knight, Nigel Stock and Frith Banbury, who would later become a noted theatrical director. Also acting in the company was the tall and distinctive Alan Napier, a young man who over 30 years later would become popular with TV audiences playing Alfred in *Batman* starring Adam West. *Little Ol' Boy* had an incredible cast of 26 players and was produced by Muriel Pratt. After the play ended work dried up for Michael, so he returned to Southsea to join Jean.

Busman's Holiday (**RKO**): (**Left to right**) **Uncredited actor, H.F. Maltby, Norman Pierce, uncredited actor, Robert Hobbs, uncredited actor, Michael Ripper, Gus McNaughton, Isobel Scaife, Wally Patch.**

It was in June 1936 that the Rippers' child was born, a daughter whom they named Susan. After the birth Jean was concerned about paying for the maternity care since funds at this time were a little bit low. However, she would not have to worry for long as Michael was called back to the film studio owned by George Smith at Walton-on-Thames. After three days of filming with William Hartnell and Max Adrian in *Nothing Like Publicity*, Michael was able to pay off the hospital fees and Jean returned home from the hospital a relieved woman.

Between 1935-39 Michael would appear in a staggering 29 films for George Smith. Each film was distributed either by RKO Radio or Columbia. Michael also got his chances between filming to work in and audition for theatre.

He would return to the Arts Theatre in London in 1936, not as an actor, but as a stage manager. The production was called *Rich Man, Poor Man* and once again featured Frith Banbury, and also Catherine Lacey, who would later appear with Michael in Hammer's *The Mummy's Shroud*.

Michael auditioned and was accepted at the Old Vic in 1936 but was soon dropped since they could not offer Michael enough money to live

A Touch of the Moon (**RKO, 1936**): (**Left to right**) **W.T. Elwanger, David Horne and Michael Ripper.**

on. So once again he returned to the film studios at Walton. The money wasn't great, but it certainly helped him to pay his way.

Since most of his time was now spent at the film studio, in January 1937, Michael and his brother Peter, rented a flat in Chiswick, London. Later Michael's wife Jean and daughter Susan would join them at the flat and this is where they continued to live until Michael completed his film work. The films he was appearing in for George Smith were made quickly and without much care. The studio was cramped and not easy to work in.

This was the hey-day of the "Quota System" which meant you had to produce 6,000 feet of film in a 10-day schedule. It was a chance given to the studio to improve their output on a cost basis.

Michael was a regular at the studio, usually playing bit parts which included everything from crooks to small comedy roles. George Smith

Ruth Wynn-Owen, Noel Iliff and Michael Ripper in a theatrical production at The Little Theatre in Leeds, 1936.

eventually offered Michael the role of second assistant director to all the films produced. Michael accepted because it meant more money, but it was very difficult work. Michael said of these days:

> You had to work like a horse from Monday through Saturday. Sunday was most certainly a day of rest, in which you stayed in bed all day. However if you were behind schedule we'd have to work overtime. Now as well as playing bit parts in each and every film, which meant I was endlessly in and out of different costumes, I was also second assistant director and was frequently saddled

up with the rather unpleasant task of asking everyone to work overtime. I don't recall anyone ever refusing to do so. We were all involved in the process of making films. There was plenty of motivation. Sometimes tempers did fly, mine included. You just didn't know where to turn next as your mind was trying to focus on so many different things.

Michael was just about to be given the job of unit manager when the Equity union stepped in, and he had to choose between being an actor or being a technician.

Luckily for us Michael stayed with acting, even though offers were coming in from Columbia and RKO, who wanted him to join them and direct films. Michael said:

> I was trained as an actor, not a director. Directing is a hard job and something I most certainly did not want to do. You leave it to the people who are skilled to do it.

In late 1938 the film industry started going through a bad spell, so Michael once again turned his mind to the theatre. He managed to get an audition with Lord Longford, and it was here that he bumped into his old friends from the Leeds days, Jean Anderson and Peter Powell.

Powell by this time was directing most of the productions that Long-ford was producing, mostly at the Ambassadors Theatre in London. Mr. Longford offered Michael work, but he would take it on only one condition—that they pay him £7 a week. Longford accepted and Michael was soon to join the company at the Gate Theatre, Dublin, Ireland. Michael would remain in Ireland for the next eight years.

He signed off from the film industry in England in 1939 with a film called *Blind Folly* and would not return to films until 1947, by which time the production standards would be slightly higher than those of his earlier films.

Michael said of his first films:

> Even though I and everyone else worked really hard at that studio at Walton-on-Thames, most of these quickie films turned out to be rather appalling, real trash, and I was absolutely diabolical, terrible on them, and that was everybody's opinion, not just mine.

It is true that most of these short films are long forgotten and probably lost. However, Michael's next move would be a far happier and a much more exciting experience than his Walton days. He waved good-bye to his wife Jean and daughter Susan, and took himself off to the Gate Theatre, Dublin, Ireland. This was the home of many fledgling actors who would later reach full maturity.

1947 portrait

Michael Ripper

Gate Theatre

It was January 1939 and WWII was looming on the horizon. Even though war was a possibility in England, Michael and Jean decided that it would be a good idea for him to go to Ireland and join Lord Longford and his theatre company. On his arrival in Dublin, his first job was to find some accommodation where he would be able to stay at least for a few months.

Another actor in the Longford company was in the same boat, so they decided to look for a room together. They finally found a flat in Dublin which they could just happily afford. So, after a short search, Michael moved into his new accommodation with Peter Copley, an old friend from his Leeds days.

Copley recalled:

> We found a top floor, small roomed flat, in a fine 18th-century house in Upper Ely Place, Dublin. The owner was an elderly grand dame, who doubted the reliability of actors, and it took many visits with Mike and me, neatly dressed and courtly in manner and unbearably patient before she accepted us. Even though we had to be well behaved at all times, because she would peep at us through a slightly open door as we climbed the handsome open staircase. We even had a young gentle girl to come and clean for a tiny sum. One day she fainted, she came from a poor house and was starving. We were appalled because she was always smiling, and never complained. Our salaries controlled our expenses, and we shopped cautiously. Mike introduced me to Black Pudding, a wonderful staple.

The company at the Gate Theatre was set up so that half the year they would perform at the Gate, and the other half would be spent on tour. For touring the acting troupe used a van, which was driven on many

Michael Ripper as the auctioneer in *Yahoo* at the Gate Theatre in Dublin, 1939.

occasions by Jean Anderson. Some of the first plays Michael appeared in were *Yahoo*, which was scripted by Longford and in which Michael played the bit part of an auctioneer; Christopher Marlowe's *Dr. Faustus*; and *A Murder Has Been Arranged*, a play written by Michael's old chum Emlyn Williams.

Michael Ripper with Cathleen Delany in *The Strange Lover* at the Gate Theatre, 1939.

The first season of plays were mostly successful and enjoyed by actors and audiences alike. The Gate Theatre's regular audience was a friendly bunch of theatre-goers, and Michael enjoyed very much performing for them. Peter Powell's direction of the plays was always first rate and his fellow company members could not have been better. The group of thespians included Michael Ripper, Anderson and Copley, Noel Iliff, Cathleen Delany, Ronald Ibbs and Dermot Kelly.

Kelly along with his wife Jill would become close friends of Michael and the friendship would last until Dermot's death many, many years later. "Dermot was a fine Irish actor, and always such a jolly cheerful man," Michael remembered, "and it was always an absolute joy to work opposite him at the Gate." Jill Kelly remembers the two actors enjoying each other's company, and even though after the Gate the two of them would only work together one more time, they still kept in constant touch. When Dermot passed away Michael said of him, "I have lost a real true friend."

Michael Ripper as Faulkland in *The Rivals* at the Gate Theatre, 1939.

Whenever he could, Michael would travel home to see Jean and Susan in Southsea. However, these infrequent once a week meetings were cut short when war was finally declared between England and Germany by Sir Winston Churchill.

Upon hearing the news of the outbreak of war, Michael decided it would be a good idea to approach the British Embassy in Dublin and ask if he should do the decent thing for his country and join up. The Embassy was not in favor of this, and Michael found their response something of a shock. The Embassy told him, "We know you're here, so you can stay put." So he returned to the Gate and his accommodation with Peter Copley.

Even though Michael continued in his season of plays for Longford, he was worried about the safety of Jean and Susan who were still living in England. It didn't make things easier for him since he could not get over to see them. However, his mind was soon put at ease when he was able to obtain a ticket for Jean and Susan to cross to Ireland and the family was at last reunited in Dublin. The crossing was somewhat ghastly but Jean and Susan did arrive in Dublin safely, if somewhat green from sea-sickness. Michael was delighted to see them both safely out of England. The entire Ripper family would remain in Dublin during the war years.

At first the family stayed in the flat, but eventually Michael managed to find another place for them to stay just outside Dublin. The new home was a lodge, attached to a farmhouse. It was a very cheerful time for Susan as she would enjoy many happy days playing on the farm and watching the animals.

Jean Anderson, Michael's colleague at the Gate, became a good friend of Michael's wife. Anderson also had a young daughter, so the two ladies would go for long walks and have chats about family life and the children.

At the theatre a different play was being performed weekly. Lord Longford kept things moving along, and Peter Powell continued directing.

Longford himself was a somewhat stout man, who had a good eye for business. On the lighter side, if you can call it that, he drove a car with a special suspension to hold his rather large frame and weight.

"Working at the Gate was a truly exciting experience," Michael remembered:

Longford was a great businessman, even though he could be quite difficult at times. Powell seemed to have a knack for making things work, even though he had to work on a tight schedule, and sometimes he and Longford would clash. Saying that though, they were good friends, we were all good friends. It was a fine company.

Jean Anderson would often play the leading ladies, she recalled:

It wasn't quite as glamorous as it sounds. The costumes were not washed enough, and often not kept in the best of places. They would begin to smell quite badly. I was supposed to be the beautiful leading lady, but smelling most appallingly. I felt sorry for my male colleagues like Michael, who had to play the leading man.

However, Anderson was a very talented lady and Michael remembers working with her with great affection. He recalled:

You honestly didn't have time to worry about smelly costumes, you were more worried about remembering your lines.

Each night after the performance had finished, the entire company would go to the local pub and taste the Guinness. "Some fun nights, and lots of laughs were had in that local boozer," Michael recalled.
But in England the war was in full force. Michael said:

We saw nothing of the war being in Ireland, but my brother Peter was in the Royal Air Force, so he was in the thick of it. I must say that I felt quite bad for not being involved in some way. But there was not much I could do about that, as I had been told to stay put by the British Embassy.

Transport in Ireland at this time was not good, and it was almost impossible to buy a car. So Michael turned to a bicycle, which he would use to cycle the four miles from his home to the Gate each day.

It was now the late summer of 1939 and some of the company members decided it was time to move on to other things. Among those departing were Anderson, Powell and Copley. Michael remembered this was a great loss to the company, and he was sorry to see them go.

Peter Copley from the *Father Brown* series (1974)

Today Anderson and Copley have similar memories of working with Michael at the Gate. Jean Anderson said of Michael:

> The one thing I remember most about working with him was his magic hands. He could express as much through his hands as he could through his voice. Almost like a mime-artist. He was a very clever and giving actor, and each and every character he played was so different. I have happy memories of working with him, and admire him a lot. But most of all I shall never forget his magic hands.

Peter Copley recalled:

> As an actor, Mike gave many fine performances, I remember him especially as Faulkland in *The Rivals* and Firs in *The Cherry Orchard*. He had a taut, well-controlled body, and quick, neat, hand and arm movements. He did unique make-ups, thick, detailed, excellent in every way, except that they covered only face and chin, and stopped with a hard line along his jaw-bone, so his collar was never dirtied. As a person, Mike could be silent and seem censorious, despite a lovely sense of humor. His flick of cigarette ash carried quiet, firm criticism.

Michael Ripper as "Hamlet the Gate Theatre.

For the next three years Michael continued acting at the Gate. His work as an actor got stronger and stronger, and the local press always gave him good reviews. The regular audience became fond of the young Ripper and looked forward to his weekly performances. He became a different character every week, with each character beccomming better than the last, and his performances were always strong and memorable.

In time he graduated to leading roles—Lord Longford had finally begun to notice his talent. One leading role however became more memorable than any other thanks to Longford, who cast him in the part knowing full well that it would show off the young Ripper's ability.

In 1943 Michael was handed the script of *Hamlet*—he was to play the title role. Michael knew it would be a challenge—he had never played a leading role in Shakespeare—but he accepted the role of Hamlet with open arms. At last he was being given the chance to play an important leading role and, not just any role, but in one of the finest plays ever written. At home, he studied the part, intensely learning the complex lines, and then reading them aloud so he could get the meaning of the words across. Michael's daughter Susan remembers:

Whenever my father reached for the text of *Hamlet* and I could hear him speaking his lines, I used to put my coat on and I was gone.

The very young Susan would go out and play. She did not like to see her father in full flight, throwing out sometimes quite powerful lines of dialogue.

Michael's own memories of playing Hamlet are very strong. "It was the best piece of theatre acting I ever did." He recalls:

Michael Ripper

Michael Ripper as Hamlet in the Gate Theatre production,1943.

I remember being quite surprised at how well I learned
the part, as I had never played a role of such great length
previously, and most definitely not a Shakespeare. Each

and every night I thoroughly enjoyed playing the role. Out of all the things I've done in the theatre, my performance as Hamlet is the one I remember the most, and the performance out of all the ones I have done that I was most pleased with.

His Hamlet most certainly did not go unnoticed—the local press gave him good reviews, and a local artist even had a drawing printed of him playing the part in a local newspaper.

Someone who will never forget Michael's performance in Hamlet was John Looby, who was 13 years old at the time. He recalls:

Michael was superb, if you can accept the judgment of a 13-year-old. Our teacher had told us that we should see it, and so three of us solemnly trooped off to a Saturday matinee, only to be told that it was sold out. We replied that we had to see it, as we had been instructed by our teacher to see it. Lord Longford himself happened to be passing, was amused by our seriousness, and decreed that see it we should, even if it meant we had to sit on the floor to the side of the stage. After seeing his wonderful, physical and energetic performance, I feel sad that I missed the period when Michael played there regularly.

Today John Looby is a good friend of Michael's and has been for over 20 years.

After *Hamlet* Michael's days at the Gate were limited, and he would not play another leading role.

He eventually made the decision to move on, and announced to Lord Longford that he would like to leave. So after five years at the Gate, Michael packed his bags and left the theatre for the final time.

The year was 1944 and Michael's move to other things would still keep him in Dublin—his next job offer would be at the Theatre Royal, just a small distance from the Gate.

Here he would not appear in straight plays, but be given his chance to appear in variety and musical comedies. "It was certainly different from *Hamlet*, or any other theatre productions I had done," Michael remembered.

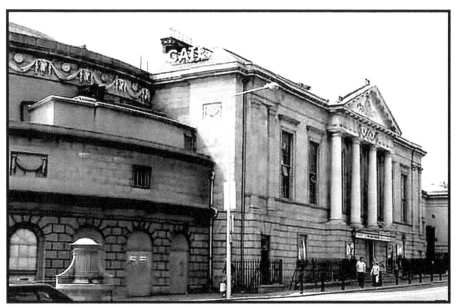
Gate Theatre in Dublin

Sometimes I would sing and dance. Now I wasn't a bad dancer but couldn't really sing, I could put over a song, but to be honest it was not a strong point. I liked watching people who could sing.

At the same time Michael was at the Theatre Royal, Eamon Andrews was presenting a quiz show at the theatre called *Double or Nothing*.

At the Gaiety Theatre, which was also in Dublin, Michael appeared in two separate productions of the famous musical *Show Boat*, but sadly for him this would also include singing. In the second production of *Show Boat*, one of the leading ladies who played opposite Michael kindly gave his daughter Susan two books on nature, which she tells me she still has today.

It was also in Ireland that Michael would give his first, and only performance in pantomime. The production was *Babes in the Wood* at the Theatre Royal, and Michael played one of the robbers. His wife Jean and daughter Susan went to see one of the performances. Susan recalls:

You know how they get children up on the stage, well, I went up, and my father looked at me, but didn't recognize me at first until I said who I was. He went off the stage and stood in the wings watching me like a hawk, it was quite funny.

When he had time off, Michael would travel back and forth from Ireland to London for auditions. He had traded up from his bicycle and would use his trusty old Fiat, crossing with it on a ferry to England.

On one occasion however he had a slight problem. His daughter Susan takes up the story:

> My father was driving behind a lorry [truck], which drove through red lights; now being directly behind he was unaware that a red light was showing, and so continued following the lorry. Unfortunately for him the police were nearby and saw this, caught my father and let the lorry escape. Anyway a solicitor ended up going to court in his place, as my father was back in London. A little while after this a policeman knocked at my mother's door and wanted to know if my father was here, and she said no he's over the other side (England). So anyway the police had a summons for two pounds which mother wasn't going to pay, and she said she wasn't sure when my father would be back. Apparently if he was away for longer than six weeks the police couldn't claim the summons. My mother said she was sure he would be away much longer than that. At which the policeman said, well you claim it from him and you can keep it.

It was now the early part of 1947 and the Rippers' marriage was going through a very bad patch; in fact it would never recover.

Michael's work in Ireland came to an end and he would never return. Eight years had passed since he first set foot in Ireland and he was reluctant to say good-bye. With his marriage in a mess, it was most definitely time for a change, but it wouldn't be easy. Michael recalled:

> Dublin leaves happy memories for me. Some of my best work and memories remain there, I was sad when I had to leave it all behind.

On his return to England he found himself a new home, Flat 4, 47 Linden Gardens in Kensington, London. His 13-year marriage was over, and a divorce was settled.

Within months he found himself a new love, a young Irish actress whom he had met in Ireland. So Catherine Finn became his new lady companion, but marriage, at least for the time being, was not in the cards.

Michael talked to his agent about possible re-entry into motion pictures, since film production in England at this time was going full force.

After a brief wait he met film director Frank Launder, a man who would go on to direct Michael in several classic British pictures. Launder would also become a close friend, and later a neighbor of Michael's. This director would give Michael a chance to show off his talents in movies, especially his comedic talents.

In 1947 Michael would sign a contract which would re-enter him into motion pictures after an eight-year absence. But this time the films would be on a far bigger budget than the ones he had made at Walton-on-Thames in the 1930s. They would also give Michael better parts. It would be a new start, and one he was more than happy to accept.

Film Greats

Captain Boycott was the first in a long line of classic British pictures in which Michael would appear. Filmed on location and at Pinewood Studios in Iver, England, it boasted an impressive cast list which included Stewart Granger, Cecil Parker, Robert Donat and Michael's old acquaintance, Alastair Sim.

In the film Michael has a small but interesting role, sharing most of his scenes with actor Noel Purcell.

The story centers on a group of landowners headed by Stewart Granger, who was at this time one of England's top stars. The Irish landowners are trying to save their families and friends from eviction by Captain Boycott, played rather comically by Cecil Parker. Michael portrays landowner Pat Nolan.

The film is a fine production and brilliantly directed by Frank Launder. "It was a fun movie to work on," Michael recalled.

> Frank Launder became a friend of mine later on, and so did his producer Sidney Gilliat. In fact between them they would both be responsible for giving me some good parts in some pretty good films. My part in *Captain Boycott* was only small, and I had very little to say, but I did appear in a good many scenes, most of the time sporting an angry face.

Of his fellow co-stars, Michael said:

> Noel Purcell was great, he looked after me on that film, we both had a lot of laughs. One of my first scenes on the film was a big one with many actors and extras. It was a

The cast of *Captain Boycott* (General Film, 1947)*:* (Back Row, left to right) Maurice Denham, Jim Philan, Liam Gaffney, Brian Smith, Noel Purcell, Eddie Golden; (Second Row) Michael Ripper, John McDarby, Liam Redmond, Eddie Byrne, Niall MacGinnis; (Third Row) Mervyn Johns, Caven Malone, Kathleen Ryan, director Frank Launder, Maureen Delaney, Bernadette O'Farrell, Alastair Sim; (Front Row Seated) Cecil Parker and Stewart Granger.

set at Pinewood and actor Robert Donat had to deliver a big speech from a stand. He was quite a big star and the delivery of his speech was amazing. I remember being taken aback by him because he was so good, and in many ways I learned a lot from watching him. Sadly though, I never got to know him personally as he was only on the set a short while and I never worked with him again. But his performance in that film does certainly stand out.

However Donat is not the only one with a stand-out scene. Michael was lucky enough to have one himself. During an important sequence in a bustling tavern, rowdy landowners are planning to take revenge and justice into their own hands after one of their friends is murdered. Michael is given his chance to shine for a few seconds, and light up the screen he certainly does. Bursting through the crowd to the front of the room he delivers the following line with powerful conviction:

Michael Ripper as Pat Nolan with Noel Purcell and Harry Webster in *Captain Boycott* **(General Film).**

> There's murder been done, one of us has been killed. Are
> we going to let that happen and not answer?

This is certainly Michael's best line in the film, and he made sure to deliver it with everything he had.

Frank Launder, who first noticed the talent of the young Ripper, would cast him in many of his films in the future.

Michael remembers:

> Stewart Granger was a nice guy, well he was to me. We
> got on very well during filming and I remember after
> one of my few lines of dialogue he came to pat me on the
> shoulder and said well done to me.

This was unusual for Granger as he very rarely complimented other actors.

Alastair Sim plays Father McKeogh in the film. Michael said:

> We spoke only a few times during filming. He was never
> an easy man to approach, and very rarely made approaches
> towards me. I knew where he got this from, he was very
> much like my father, extremely reserved. However, say-
> ing this, he was never unfriendly towards me when I did
> actually approach him for a chat.

Another actor in the film was veteran character actor Maurice Denham playing the part of Lt. Col. Strickland. Denham recalled Frank
Launder:

> Launder was a marvelous director. If he liked what you
> showed him, he'd let you do it. The enjoyment of making
> a film is 89 percent there if you have a good director, and
> Launder was a good director to be around.

Maurice Denham would go on to appear in several films that Michael was in, but the two actors would never share the same scenes.

After *Captain Boycott* Michael made a brief but welcome return to the theatre. The play was called *Boys in Brown* by Reginald Beckwith. The play premiered at the Arts Theatre, London, in May 1947, and then transferred to the Duchess Theatre, London, in July of the same year.

Produced by Norman Marshall, the action of the play is set in a Borstal Institution. Michael played the part of Casey. He said:

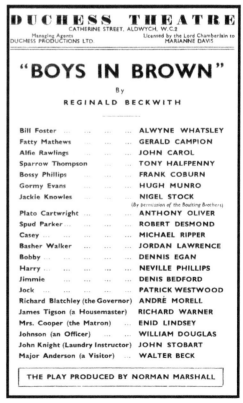

DUCHESS THEATRE

CATHERINE STREET, ALDWYCH, W.C.2

Managing Agents
DUCHESS PRODUCTIONS LTD.

Licensed by the Lord Chamberlain to
MARIANNE DAVIS

"BOYS IN BROWN"

By

REGINALD BECKWITH

Bill Foster	ALWYNE WHATSLEY
Fatty Mathews	GERALD CAMPION
Alfie Rawlings	JOHN CAROL
Sparrow Thompson	TONY HALFPENNY
Bossy Phillips	FRANK COBURN
Gormy Evans	HUGH MUNRO
Jackie Knowles	NIGEL STOCK
	(By permission of the Boulting Brothers)
Plato Cartwright	ANTHONY OLIVER
Spud Parker	ROBERT DESMOND
Casey	MICHAEL RIPPER
Basher Walker	JORDAN LAWRENCE
Bobby	DENNIS EGAN
Harry	NEVILLE PHILLIPS
Jimmie	DENIS BEDFORD
Jock	PATRICK WESTWOOD
Richard Blatchley (the Governor)	ANDRÉ MORELL
James Tigson (a Housemaster)	RICHARD WARNER
Mrs. Cooper (the Matron) ...	ENID LINDSEY
Johnson (an Officer)	WILLIAM DOUGLAS
John Knight (Laundry Instructor)	JOHN STOBART
Major Anderson (a Visitor) ...	WALTER BECK

THE PLAY PRODUCED BY NORMAN MARSHALL

I remember it being quite controversial for its time as it tackled a rather difficult subject. Today though it's probably rather tame.

Also in the cast was an actor whom Michael would meet many times in the future, Andre Morell. Michael remembers:

It was the first time I ever worked with him. I always found him to be a very strong performer, and his part of The Governor in *Boys in Brown* was no exception. It was always a pleasure to work with him, and when he wasn't acting he was very gentlemanly and polite.

This particular production would also give Michael his first chance to appear on television. Back then there was only BBC TV, still in its infancy. They were interested in broadcasting *Boys in Brown* using the original cast. Producer Michael Barry took charge of the production and rehearsals began on July 23, 1947 at St. Hilda's Convent, Maida Vale, in London. Michael recalls:

We rehearsed for four days. Rehearsals, especially in the early days of TV, always took place in not the cleanest of places. On the day of performance we rehearsed all day at Alexandra Palace in London, a huge Victorian pile which had been turned into the BBC studios. It was always a pleasant atmosphere whenever I worked at that big old building. The performance for *Boys in Brown* started at 8:30 p.m. on July 27, 1947. You did get slightly nervous as it was live TV, so this meant you didn't get a second take. You just had to treat it like a theatre performance and hope it went right. I don't remember anything going badly wrong, it wouldn't have made much difference if things had. Very few people could afford TV sets in those days, and I always remember that at the end of a broadcast you would bow like in the theatre as if the curtain was going in and out. I did find this most amusing, but they did eventually get rid of it. Technically for the crew it must have been a pain trying not to get lights, boom mikes and cameras into shot during transmission. The whole thing

Michael Ripper as Casey in *Boys in Brown* at the Duchess Theatre, 1947.

was certainly an experience for me and set me in good
stead for other live TV work in the future.

After the TV experience Michael found himself once again back at the
Arts Theatre, London. It was also a reunion for him with his old friend

Jean Anderson, who was acting in the play which was being produced by none other than her husband, Peter Powell.

The play was called *Pride Shall Have a Fall.* Michael and Jean depicted Count and Countess Ventoso.

The theatre reunion with Jean and Peter was short lived, and Michael soon found himself back in the film studio. Small parts followed in films like *Noose* in which Michael played the part of Nelson, and a brief but interesting role in David Lean's outstanding version of *Oliver Twist.*

Michael remembers his time on the film:

My first day on set was with Robert Newton who was playing Bill Sykes. He was very good in that part; I played Barney his helper. I remember being quite frightened of Newton as he was a very striking actor, his eyes kind of burnt into you, and he used every look to full effect when playing that part of Sykes. Alec Guinness was there too, but inside all that incredible make-up he was totally unrecognizable as Fagin. Now Guinness to me has got to be one of our finest character actors, his part as Fagin proves that. The film itself is visually stunning thanks to David Lean's direction and Guy Green's superb photography. Lean as a director was perfectionism at its best, and the amount of physical energy he put into directing a scene was incredible. It could be tough at times, but he knew what he wanted and he got it every time. He and Guy

Green invented some incredible photographic images on that movie. The ending of the film set in Fagin's den is one of the best I think ever captured on screen. During this scene a big wooden door had to be broken through which I was directly on the other end of with several other actors. The actors on the other side of the door broke through with such force that the bloody thing nearly ended up on top of me and it was very heavy strong wood. That was another thing about that movie. The set pieces were brilliantly designed and constructed. Well, what do you expect, it was a David Lean movie. I am very proud to have been part of it.

During the summer of 1948 Michael was contacted by Alastair Sim who wanted him to play a part in his forthcoming play at Westminster Theatre in London. Michael noted:

I found it rather strange as he never contacted me, so what made him on this occasion? It was odd that Alastair always seemed to turn up at unusual moments. Like for instance when I bumped into him in London in the 1930s and he was more or less responsible for my start in films. It was as if he was guiding my career. Perhaps my father was talking to him. Anyway I never found out.

Alastair offered Michael the part of Hare the bodysnatcher in the play *The Anatomist* about resurrection men in Edinburgh over a century ago. Alastair Sim played Dr. Knox, a lecturer in anatomy and patron of Burke and Hare. Sim was also director of the play which opened at the Westminster in November 1948. Michael said of his time in the production:

It was very enjoyable, especially playing a bodysnatcher, my first real horror role. Sim directed the play with great pace, but once again I never managed to get very close to him as a friend.

Even though Michael enjoyed his stint on the play it got mixed reviews. One reviewer from *The Times* said:

Mr. Sim was often inaudible and the rest of the cast showed a tendency to gabble. Mr. George Cole as the young Doctor and the Burke and Hare of Mr. Liam Redmond and Mr. Michael Ripper are the strongest of a weak cast.

One can only wonder what Sim thought of reviews such as this with other actors, including Ripper, upstaging him. Michael would never be employed by Sim again.

During the run of *The Anatomist* Liam Redmond had to leave and the part of Burke was then taken over by Ian Wallace. Like *Boys in Brown* before it, this production was also broadcast by BBC television. It went out live from Alexandra Palace on January 23, 1949 at 8:30 p.m. It had the same cast with the exception of the Burke character. However, this time the change was met with Michael's

Michael Ripper as Hare with Dermot Kelly in *The Anatomist* (BBC Television, 1949).

full approval. Added to the cast was his dear old friend Dermot Kelly. Michael stated:

> We worked really well together in that. I enjoyed playing the part to start with, but to have Dermot playing opposite me was an added bonus, it was marvelous.

This TV broadcast is lost and it would be the final time Dermot and Michael would work together.

Whenever he had free time Michael would travel to see his daughter Susan. Today he looks back and gives his own thoughts of visiting his daughter at this time:

> Oh I loved her all right. She was great, and I tried to show as much love towards her as I possibly could. I would never have dreamed of hitting her. Because under no circumstances did I want to be like my father had been to me.

In 1949 Michael appeared in two films produced by John Mills and directed by Anthony Pelissier. The films were *The History of Mr. Polly* and *The Rocking Horse Winner*. Michael remembers working on these films:

> I had tiny roles in both, but it was an enormous pleasure to work with John Mills, a really nice guy who was a big star even at that time. He had just completed *Scott of the Antarctic*.

John Mills and John Howard Davies in *The Rocking Horse Winner*

It was not long after this that Michael got what he hoped would be his big break in Robert Montgomery's *Your Witness* but, as we already know, it came to nothing. In fact, today that film is very rarely shown, almost a lost Ripper performance—a real shame since Montgomery, who had become a good friend of Michael's during filming, was giving Michael his chance to shine in a leading role. Montgom-

Studio photograph of Michael Ripper with Robert Montgomery for *Your Witness* **(Warner Bros., 1950).**

ery had obviously noticed a talent in Michael. Michael remembered Montgomery:

> Montgomery was a true Hollywood star. We got on very well indeed. He told me wonderful stories between takes about working with John Wayne and other Hollywood greats. It's a shame we never got the chance to work together again.

Actress Jenny Laird plays Michael's wife in the picture. She recalls:

> I found Robert and Michael very pleasant to work with. Michael and I actually did very few scenes together on that film, most of my scenes were with Robert. I remember sitting with Robert at the side of the set, Michael was there

Michael Ripper as Jake with Arthur Lucan and Sebastian Cabot in *Old Mother Riley's Jungle Treasure* **(Renown Films, 1951).**

too, I think. Anyway Robert told us he was thinking of going into this new television medium. This I viewed with some disdain coming from a big film star! He saw ahead where I didn't. But I remember we all got on very well.

In the film Michael gives a solid performance, and you would think that a leading role in a Warner Bros. movie would have given Michael's film career a boost. But instead his calling fell back a notch, and Michael found himself back at the Walton-on-Thames film studio where he began his film career in the 1930s. He was also reunited with a director he had made several films with during that period—his old colleague Maclean Rogers. Michael was back at Walton to appear in *Old Mother Riley's Jungle Treasure* and was cast as a villain named Jake.

The character Mother Riley was created by music hall artiste Arthur Lucan, who had played the old washerwoman on stage and screen for a large part of his life. His wife, Kitty Mcshane, always appeared alongside him playing Mother Riley's daughter (called, surprisingly enough, Kitty). When speaking of this film Michael observes:

I remember Lucan being around when I was at Walton in the 1930s. But I never had anything to do with him because I wasn't in his films. He was playing Mother Riley even then. This character Lucan had created was ingenious and very funny. Mother Riley for Lucan was a very physical part, and he went into it with immense energy. His arms and legs were like wires and once he started throwing them around there was no stopping him. When I worked with him though he was quite an old man, he used to sweat heavily during scenes and become tired quite quickly. Kitty used to fuss around him and help him in and out of his costume. As a person Lucan seemed to be an unhappy man at this time in his life. He always looked sad. Perhaps I'm wrong but that's how I saw it. Both he and Mcshane were very private people whom I didn't get to know that well. I was only actually working on that film a few days anyway. But to have worked with Lucan in what was to me one of his last films was a treat, and I shall always remember that out of this unhappy, sad looking man sprang Mother Riley, so full of life and very jolly and silly.

More films were to follow and he also did more live broadcasts from Alexandra Palace for the BBC. One of these was playing the title role in *The Strange Case of Hans Krantzer*.

On March 16, 1952 Michael was back on the stage appearing in the play *World Without End*. His co-stars were husband and wife Dermot Walsh and Hazel Court. Michael said, "Hazel and Dermot were great fun to be around, such a smashing couple. I was quite surprised when they split some years later as they seemed so happy."

PREVIEW THEATRE CLUB

present

World Without End

by

WILLIAM RANSTED BERRY

Cast in order of their appearance:

Napoleon Bonaparte	...	...	MICHAEL RIPPER
Kaiser William II	...	...	ERIC MESSITER
Attila, King of the Huns	...		ALEXANDER FIELD
Alexander the Great	...		RICHARD CURNOCK (by courtesy of Jack de Leon)
Julius Cæsar	...	...	... IVAN SAMSON
Hetty Norton	...	...	... JOAN YOUNG
Joe Norton ...	...	...	DERMOT WALSH (by courtesy of Rix Theatrical Productions)
Manuel Silva	...	...	... JOHN SLATER
Orin Hewett	...	...	... JON FARREL
Susie Osborne	...	...	... HAZEL COURT
Clem Osborne	...	...	... JOHN KIRCH
A Messenger	...	...	... CARL RAYNOR

Directed by HUGH CROSS
Sets by MICHAEL LACEY and HUGH CROSS
Costumes by MICHAEL LACEY
Music Arranged by LYDIA RAGOSIN

To the administrators and staff of the Fortune and Scala Theatres, without whose enthusiasm and co-operation our task in presenting this play would have been immeasurably more difficult, the Preview Theatre Club tender their most sincere thanks.

The play ran its course at the Fortune Theatre, London, but was not a great success.

During the summer of 1952 Michael had to go to the hospital for what turned out to be a serious thyroid and throat operation. Michael takes up the story:

> I was having a bit of trouble and the next thing I was in hospital about to undergo a serious operation. It was this operation on my throat that put a stop to my theatre career, as voice projection of a big kind after this was almost impossible. In fact I was unable to speak well at all after that, and for many months I didn't really sound like a human being.

However things were not all bad—Michael was able to return to film work and appeared in six feature films in 1952 alone, and he did have the chance to appear in another theatrical production many years later.

When leaving the hospital the doctor told Michael that any serious shock to his system could be fatal. These were quite harsh words so Michael decided it would be a good idea to relax and put his feet up for a few weeks. On one of those relaxing days he decided to go along to an Air Show. This day of relaxation turned into a horrific tragedy. It was September 1952 and Michael decided to attend the Farnborough Air Show in Hampshire. He was among 150,000 people watching the display that day when disaster struck. The De Havilland 110 Fighter was giving its performance when the plane suddenly hurtled out of control, flew downward and hit part of the crowd with tremendous speed. Michael recalls this terrible day:

> It was horrible. Possibly the worst day of my life. You see the plane came down so quick, nobody was expecting it. I remember it hit a crowd of people and exploded. It was devastating. I was actually a good distance from where this happened because an enormous crowd had turned out that day. People were screaming and in shock. I was stunned, as I had never witnessed anything like it before. I do remember that over 20 people lost their lives, and many more were injured. It's quite frightening

Air show horror kills 28

Part of the disintegrated D.H.110 hits the ground in an explosion of debris.

really, that a happy day out turned into a nightmare for a lot of people.

The doctor had told Michael that any shock could be fatal. He had possibly the biggest shock of his life that day but luckily was unaffected.

Michael continued his film career and in one of his next roles he played a decent part opposite actor Maurice Evans in *The Story of Gilbert and Sullivan*. Michael played Louis, manservant to Evans' character. Michael remembers:

> It was a very colorful film, and mine was a good part. I had to follow Evans about a lot, dress him, answer the phone. It had a good cast including Robert Morley and Peter Finch. Maurice Evans was all right, but like Morley and Finch, he very much kept himself to himself, so I didn't know any of them well. You would think with me playing a good part we would all be good friends. But

to be honest getting to know those three actors was a bit like getting to know the Pope. Morley seemed to be quite jolly, when I saw him that is.

The film was directed by Sidney Gilliat who had been producer on Michael's earlier film *Captain Boycott*.

Michael's work in films continued and several of these are stand out productions.

In 1954 Michael appeared in the first of four famous comedy films about a girls' school called St. Trinian's. All four were directed by Frank Launder, and the first in the series was *The Belles of St. Trinian's* in which Michael played the character Albert Faning.

This film was followed by an appearance in a classic war film *The Sea Shall Not Have Them* with Michael Redgrave and Dirk Bogarde, directed by Lewis Gilbert. Michael said:

> About all I remember about that film is that we had an appalling location. It was Felixstowe in Suffolk out of season. Don't go there out of season. Oh yes, and my old mate Michael Balfour was in it, and it was always a great pleasure to work with him.

Michael's next role was playing the Left Luggage Attendant in the film *The Constant Husband*. He recalls:

> That was filmed at Shepperton Studios. It was with Rex Harrison and Kay Kendall. Now she was a very attractive lady. Tall and dark, very lively and extremely polite and well mannered. She and Rex, if I remember, seemed to be in love at that time. Well Rex was always a real charmer anyway.

Michael's next part would become his favorite:

> I was in *Richard III*, it was the best film I was ever in. I had a good part and it was a great film. Laurence Olivier directed and played Richard. Olivier was really good to me, a really nice man. Energy was number one with him and he always got good performances from his actors.

Michael Ripper relaxing on the set of *The Belles of St. Trinian's* (British Lion, 1954).

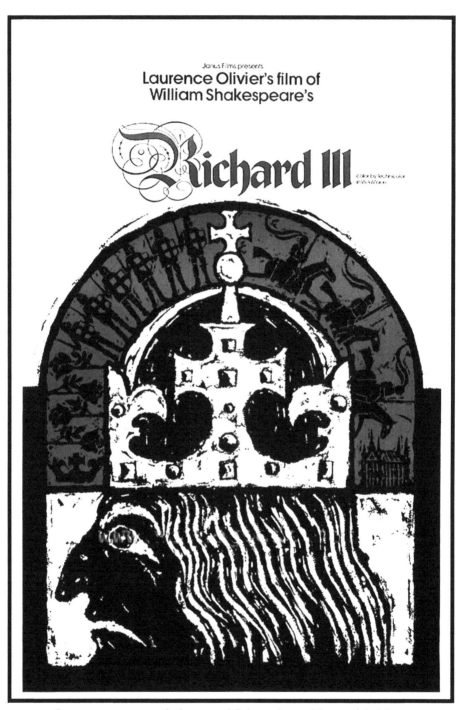

Janus Films presents
Laurence Olivier's film of
William Shakespeare's

Richard III

Color by Technicolor
in VistaVision

It was a treasured time and I loved working with him.
For such a big star he was extremely friendly and I must
admit that I was quite surprised at this. Sir John Gielgud

Michael Ripper

was also in my scenes. Sir John was also a gentlemen of
the first rank. Both he and Olivier, possibly the greatest
actors in the world, would be knighted and become Sirs,
much deserved. What more can I say, a marvelous film,
two great actors, I had the time of my life. The trouble
is, it was all too brief.

In the film Michael played the part of the second murderer. Playing Dighton the first murderer was another great English actor, Michael
Gough. The two actors had a scene in which they had to murder Sir John
Gielgud's character and stuff him into a vat of wine. Michael Gough
recalls:

> All I remember of *Richard III* is that me and Michael
> Ripper had great difficulty stuffing Sir John Gielgud's
> stand-in into a vat of wine, and we had several days of
> retakes, which I must say was very handy for the school
> fees and the mortgage.

Sir John Gielgud had no memories of this. He said:

> It was a long time ago and the studio always very full
> of people. I am nearly 94 so my memory is somewhat
> intermittent.

Perhaps Sir John didn't want to remember this particular incident!
Michael's next film, *Reach For the Sky* with Kenneth More saw
Michael playing an airplane mechanic. Michael said:

> Whenever I saw an airplane it brought back those horrible
> memories of Farnborough. To think that such an incred-
> ible invention, a magnificent machine, is not without its
> faults.

In *The Green Man*, made in 1956, Michael found himself acting one
last time with Alastair Sim. Michael remembers:

> Alastair was a lot friendlier towards me on the set of that
> film, he seemed different. I noticed him watching me

off set when I was doing my scene with actor Raymond Huntley. It wasn't the first time I had noticed him doing this though. I remember him coming to me and wishing me luck in the future. All I could think was what a strange thing to say, anyway, it was most unlike him. It was the last time we met and worked together. I never bumped into him again.

Following this film Michael worked in a film which gave Diana Dors an absorbing role as a Ruth Ellis–type murderess who ends up being sentenced to death. The film was *Yield to the Night*. Michael, as Roy, is desperate to have Dors go on a date with him, but each time he is turned down. He reminisces:

> It was a good film. Dors was excellent. She was very glamorous at that time, but very down to earth, a lovely person. The glamour was for the films, she knew what she was doing all right. We were good friends at one time.

Next up was a film with Ronald Shiner set onboard a ship. This farce was called *Not Wanted on Voyage*. Michael recalls:

> Shiner, if I remember rightly, was responsible for casting me in that film. He was a very funny man and acting with him and trying to keep a straight face was almost impossible. He'd desperately try and give you the giggles and succeeded nearly every time. Brian Rix was on that film as well. It was good fun.

Michael appeared in another film with Shiner shortly afterwards which was also set onboard a ship, a comedy called *Girls at Sea*. This film featured an up and coming actor named Ian Holm.

Blue Murder at St. Trinian's was one of his next ventures, and in this he had a change of character from his previous St. Trinians outing.

> I became Eric, a liftman. And I stayed the same character for the two later St. Trinians films. It was really thanks to Frank Launder, as he wanted me to be a regular character. Eric, in fact, was the only part that I played in more than

Michael Ripper as Eric the liftman in *Blue Murder at St. Trinian's* (British Lion, 1957).

one film. He was a good, enjoyable, fun part to play. Definitely a favorite of mine.

Michael looks back on his association with film director Frank Launder:

He was very friendly as far as I was concerned. We were very close at work, and he always managed to cast me very well indeed. As a director he could be a bit of a practical joker, especially with me. In fact, I remember one scene on that second St. Trinians film, I had to have a bucket of water thrown at me playing the liftman as if it were splashing out of a swimming pool. Launder himself threw that bucket of water, and I think it gave him great pleasure. It went full force into my face and was freezing cold. Thankfully we only did one take, but Launder loved every second of it. I vowed one day to get him back, but never did.

In the film Michael appears for the first time with comedy actor Terry-Thomas. Michael remembers this comedy legend:

I have worked with two comedy actors in my time whom I couldn't quite work out. One of these was Terry-Thomas. First of all, he seemed to be a deeply private man, and if he didn't know you, he'd keep away. I did a couple of scenes with him and must admit that I didn't feel 100 percent comfortable in his presence. Another one was Tony Hancock who I met later. He was another one who made you feel slightly uncomfortable and, once again, if he didn't know you he'd stay away. Hancock was a really miserable man and always looked incredibly depressed. Apparently, I was told he didn't like being upstaged. Anyway I could never have upstaged them as they were two brilliantly original comedy actors. It's a shame really that I didn't find them the easiest men to work with. They were not difficult, just deeply private, they didn't really say much to me, so sadly, it made me feel uneasy. I could be totally wrong about them both because I know a lot of people got on fine with them. Perhaps I'm just the odd one out, or maybe I just met the two great comedy actors when they were having bad days.

The film in which Michael met Tony Hancock was *The Punch and Judy Man,* filmed in 1962.

In the late 1950s, apart from film work, Michael found himself in great demand as an actor on television and appeared in some classic productions including *The Scarlet Pimpernel*, *Douglas Fairbanks Presents*, *The Invisible Man* and *Ivanhoe* with Roger Moore. One production he was offered, *A Game for Eskimos*, he felt he had to turn down. In a letter to the BBC he wrote:

> Many thanks for your kind offer, it is with much regret that I feel bound to turn it down. This chap George whom you wish me to play, seems to need more poundage than I possess. Both his wife and Paddy should be in some physical awe of him when his temper is up, and when he is in good humor, it seems to me that there should be something tidal-wave like about his antics—dancing and so forth. Perhaps some other time.

It seems strange that Michael should turn down an offer, since he was capable of playing anything as he had proved in earlier roles and would amply prove in the future. Perhaps on this one occasion he felt the character was out of his depth (or width).

Michael is the type of actor who could easily jump from one production to another, from TV to film. Some of these projects he was happy to be associated with, others he wasn't so sure about. This includes a film he appeared in called *I Only Arsked* in 1958. When asked about this he said:

> Oh my God yes, well, that was a load of old cobbler's, wasn't it? I played a mad Arab. Although I must say I enjoyed playing it.

At this point in his career Michael was unhappy about many of the parts he was being offered. In a letter to producer Michael Barry at the BBC, whom Michael had worked with previously, his agent Peter Eade wrote:

> You probably know Michael Ripper well from his many appearances in films and television films. He is now most anxious to do some TV drama. His is now over 40 and feels he doesn't want to be typed to the rather spivvy Cockney characters which he played when he was younger. He is, in fact, a good dramatic actor and played in a great many serious roles at the Gate Theatre in Dublin. Would

Live BBC version of *Quatermass and the Pit*

you suggest his name when you are discussing casting with various producers?

This letter had a very good response, and almost immediately Michael found himself appearing in one of the best-remembered television productions of his career—Rudolph Cartier's landmark science fiction cult drama series for the BBC, *Quatermass and the Pit.*

Andre Morell played the title role, and Michael's part was that of an army Sergeant. He remembers:

> It was a good part. Probably my best on early television. It was recorded live, but this time at the BBC's Riverbank Studios in Hammersmith in London. I think I did five out of the six episodes. It was an enormous success and a pretty good recording of it does actually exist on video today. Rudolph Cartier produced it and he'd been responsible for some pretty ground- breaking television productions, of which *Quatermass and the Pit* was just another one.

1958 saw Michael appear a few times in another television production which had also gained something of a cult status over the years—*The Adventures of Robin Hood* with Richard Greene playing Robin. The show featured an unforgettable signature tune many baby boomers can still hum today.

In one episode, *The Healing Hand*, Michael played Oswald, a quack doctor. It was also on this episode that Michael met a future friend, actor James Ellis. James recalls:

> My part, unlike Michael's, was a tiny one consisting of about one line, two coughs and a spit, the character did not even have a name, just "Thin Man," a role for which I would not qualify now. I certainly remember Michael being very kind and welcoming. It was filmed, I know, at Walton-on-Thames over 40 years ago, and I have received more repeat royalties for this over the years than from any other single source. It's a strange thing about our business that really nice guys often excel in really nasty roles, and Michael, his eyes twinkling with merriment just before a take, could turn on the menace with the best of them and turn the viewers' blood cold.

Michael said of the 1950s series:

> It was an enjoyable show to work on, and the finished thing always looked pretty good. Now dear old Richard Greene always cut a dashing figure as the legendary hero. But he was definitely an actor that liked to live life to the full. But you cannot blame him for that.

In 1958 a call to Michael's agent from a film company at Bray Studios in Berkshire, England, would trigger off a list of film performances for which Michael would be most remembered. This particular company would give Michael the chance to widen his scope as a character actor—Hammer Film Productions.

The Pirates of Blood River (Hammer, 1962)

Michael Ripper

Under the Hammer

In the first of his horror film appearances for Hammer Film Productions, Michael played a graverobber, Kurt. After a bit of persuasion from his drinking partner and the promise of money, he is coerced into digging up Baron Frankenstein.

That film was *The Revenge of Frankenstein*, and Fritz, his drinking partner and fellow graverobber, was played by actor Lionel Jeffries who recalls:

> I found Michael a thorough joy to work with and, as far as I remember, we laughed our way through that scene in *The Revenge of Frankenstein.* Hardly the correct behavior for two bodysnatchers.

This wasn't the first time Michael had worked for Hammer Films. He takes up the story from the beginning, leading up to Hammer's golden years:

> I remember my agent sending me to Wardour Street, London, to meet a certain James Carreras who was head of Exclusive Films Limited, which later became Hammer Films, but that was really when the horror films started. Now James, or Jimmy as I began to know him, was very welcoming, full of charm. Another young man whom I met at this time was Anthony Hinds, who would become one of my closest friends. My first film appearance for the company was in 1947, *The Dark Road* it was called, a long-forgotten film. I cannot even remember what I played in it and, to be honest, I don't care very much. My next films were a couple of *P.C. 49* films both produced

Hugh Latimer with Michael Ripper as Fingers in *The Adventures of P.C. 49* (Exclusive Films, 1949).

BRIAN REECE·JOY SHELTON
CHRISTINE NORDEN

IN

A CASE FOR P.C. 49

1   It's "Safe as Houses" Mass entertainment.—"Kine"
2   Type of entertainment which has already proved
    its Box Office worth.—"Cinema"
    A.B.C. Circuit Release, Monday, July 23rd.

by Anthony Hinds. My first decent film for the company was a short called *A Man on the Beach*. In it I played a Chauffeur and got to ride around in an old-fashioned car. Joseph Losey directed and me and Michael Medwin had a fight in a mud pit. Anyway I'm killed off in the first 10 minutes and end up getting dragged through all this mud.

Michael Ripper (face down) and Michael Medwin in *A Man on the Beach* (Hammer, 1955).

Not very pleasant, if I remember and I was wearing an
immaculate white shirt, not so immaculate after that.

Michael's next two films for the company after the *P.C. 49* series
would be on a slightly bigger scale. The first was *X—The Unknown*, a
film about radioactive ooze coming from 2,000 miles beneath the earth.
In the film Michael plays Sergeant Grimsdyke who is brought in with his
men to try to stop the deadly menace. Michael looks back at the film:

At first I thought it all sounded pretty stupid. But to be
honest the script wasn't all that bad. It was written though

The notorious pit in *X—The Unknown* (Hammer, 1956).

Michael Ripper as Sergeant Grimsdyke with John Harvey and Peter Hammond in *X—The Unknown* **(Hammer).**

Sharing a laugh on the set of *X — The Unknown* are Edwin Richfield, Anthony Newley, Ian McNaughton, Kenneth Cope and Michael Ripper.

"It was bloody freezing" during the filming of *X — The Unknown* (Hammer), Michael Ripper remarked.

by Jimmy Sangster, one of Hammer's finest screenplay writers. He also did *A Man on the Beach* before this. It was winter time when we filmed *X—The Unknown*, and most of my scenes were filmed in this muddy quarry, and it was bloody freezing.

Quatermass II was next.

The Quatermass films were very successful pictures. Hammer used to bring in American stars. It was Dean Jagger on *X—The Unknown* and for the first two Quatermass films it was Brian Donlevy. He was quite a serious man who used to drink quite heavily, whiskey I think. One day while on location near Brighton, Donlevy's toupee blew off because of the force of wind machines that were being used. The crew and Donlevy were desperately trying to save his toupee. Donlevy was not amused.

Ripper as Ernie the barman and Brian Donlevy in *Quatermass II* **(Hammer, 1957)**

Michael was not given the chance to appear in Hammer's first two highly successful horror pictures *The Curse of Frankenstein* and *Dracula* (U.S. title *Horror of Dracula*). But he did get his chance to appear in

Michael Ripper

Michael Ripper and Percy Herbert (left) battle the *Enemy from Space* (U.S. title) in *Quatermass II* (Hammer).

the sequels to these movies—*The Revenge of Frankenstein* and *Brides of Dracula*.

> I played a coachman in the latter but I don't remember much more about it because it was a very small role.

Away from the horror genre Michael appeared in comedy and war films for Hammer. In a couple of comedy films he did for the company, *Up the Creek* and *Further Up the Creek*, his appearances were so brief it was hardly worth his time.

However on the war films side of things he faired slightly better. *The Steel Bayonet* was the first in which Michael appeared with actor Leo Genn. This film was followed by *Camp on Blood Island* and a sequel several years later, *Secret of Blood Island*.

Michael looks back at the latter two:

Michael Ripper as the coachman in this eerie sequence from *Brides of Dracula* (Hammer, 1960).

The first of the two was one of the most successful films made by Hammer. It was quite a strong, powerful film for its time, dealing with the appalling Japanese P.O.W. Camps. We filmed at Bray Studios and on location at a sand quarry. Hammer seemed to have a thing about filming at quarries. Black Park near Pinewood Studios was another location. The sets at Bray were very realistic, they always were. The actual camp set with its imported palm trees couldn't have looked more like a Japanese P.O.W. Camp. The production designer's eye for detail on these movies, in particular Hammer's number one designer Bernard Robinson, was spot on. His set pieces were the real star of those movies. He was a brilliantly, incredibly

As Private Middleditch in *The Steel Bayonet* (Hammer, 1957).

clever man. The sequel to *Camp* was a bit of a disappointment. I thought the story was very dodgy, I didn't really believe that story at all. In both films I played Japanese officers. Oh God yes, can you believe it, me as a Japanese. Only Hammer would cast me as a Japanese.

Ripper and Leo Genn share a scene in *The Steel Bayonet* (Hammer).

Michael's performances in these movies are very memorable and somewhat sinister, and frightening—you never felt for one minute that he wasn't Japanese. Michael once again proved he could take on the most difficult of characters and make you believe his portrayals.

Actor Bill Owen appeared in *Secret of Blood Island*, and had this to say about Michael:

> As I am now in my 62nd year as an actor, I have to admit to difficulty trying to recall how many times Michael and

As a Japanese soldier, Ripper gleefully holds a gun on Carl Mohner in *The Camp on Blood Island* **(Hammer, 1958).**

I may have worked together. But on those rare occasions my response was always the same, as if I had known him all my life. A good man with a wry humor. One of these meetings took place with the film *Secret of Blood Island* in which Michael was cast as a Japanese Commander of a Japanese Prisoner of War Camp. Not exactly type casting, but he frightened the life out of we other "principals" playing the "inmates." Now the "extras" engaged as the other p.o.w.'s were perfect, emaciated, bent and bony, a sorry lot, but not the principal characters however. We had not received orders to starve. On the first day of shooting Michael appeared, the personification of a wicked Camp Commandant with a suitable North Finchley Japanese accent. Turning to the Director he inquired, "Please,

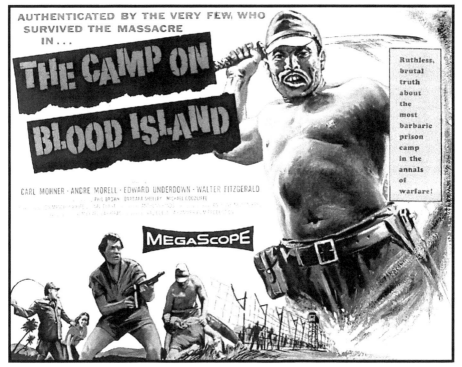

AUTHENTICATED BY THE VERY FEW, WHO SURVIVED THE MASSACRE IN . . .

THE CAMP ON BLOOD ISLAND

Ruthless, brutal truth about the most barbaric prison camp in the annals of warfare!

CARL MOHNER · ANDRE MORELL · EDWARD UNDERDOWN · WALTER FITZGERALD
PHIL BROWN · BARBARA SHELLEY · MICHAEL COOZLIFFE

MEGASCOPE

what is my attitude towards these fat prisoners of war?"
I enjoyed working with Michael.

In 1958 Michael found himself with enough money in the bank to move from his flat in Kensington, London and start building himself a new home in Chinnor, Oxfordshire, which he would call "Larkrise."

> I had a place built in the countryside. I was a lot stronger then. It was a three-bedroom bungalow with a double garage and two acres of land. One of the acres was where I grew fruits, an orchard; pears, apples and other fruits. It turned out to be a very nice place.

Sharing the new bungalow with Michael was Catherine Finn, still his partner, but not his wife. Michael's close neighbors when living in Chinnor were Frank Launder, Sidney Gilliat and Hammer's Anthony Hinds, all of whom were good friends. Anthony Hinds was a regular visitor to Michael's bungalow "Larkrise" in Chinnor. Hinds wrote the screenplay to Hammer's *The Reptile*, in which there is a little cottage called surprisingly enough "Larkrise." Chinnor was very close to Hammer's Bray Studios

Michael Ripper

THE SECRET OF BLOOD ISLAND
EASTMAN COLOUR   starring   (X)
JACK HEDLEY · BARBARA SHELLEY
PATRICK WYMARK · CHARLES TINGWELL
A HAMMER FILM PRODUCTION
FOR
UNIVERSAL-INTERNATIONAL

where Michael would continue to work on a regular basis.

His next film part for them as a drunken old poacher would become a most memorable one in the lavish and extremely expensive-looking *The Mummy*. The scene in which Michael goes into the inn after seeing

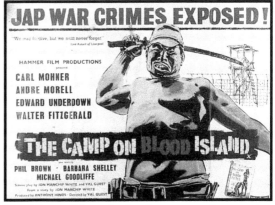

the bandaged giant is a classic. After telling the innkeeper and a regular what he's seen in the woods, the regular, played in a very dry comic manner by actor Gerald Lawson, turns to Michael and says, "Have you been seeing the little people again?" Michael, after a swig of whiskey answers, "If it's little people, it's the biggest little people you've ever heard anything about." After which he orders another whiskey. Michael said:

> Jimmy Sangster was responsible for that lovely little part
> I played in *The Mummy*. You see he wrote the script, but
> he wrote it very much with me in mind.

Ripper as the "drunken old poacher" in *The Mummy* (Hammer, 1959).

From the beginning of Hammer's cycle of horror films until their final days, only three actors appeared regularly in Hammer films—Peter Cushing, Christopher Lee and Michael Ripper (who actually appeared in more than Cushing and Lee).

Ripper shares a scene with George Pastell in *The Mummy* (Hammer).

The Mummy was the first Hammer film in which all three actors worked together.

> Poor old Christopher. He had such a bad time on that film. All that heavy make-up etc., playing the mummy. It must have been sheer hell for him. Christopher is one of my dearest friends, he always makes me laugh. In fact, I don't think he ever liked working with me because we laughed so much. I think he's a very funny fellow. Now I don't think I actually met Peter on the set of that film. I know we didn't share any scenes.

Playing the "Old Soak" in *The Curse of the Werewolf*, Michael worked for the first time with the recently deceased Oliver Reed, who was also somewhat of a regular in Hammer films. Michael recalled:

> I had a prison scene with Ollie in *The Curse of the Were-wolf*. Yes, I was locked in a cell with Ollie Reed. I've actually got a photograph from that scene, and it's Ollie in a close-up and I'm in the background looking absolutely horrified. Obviously there was good reason for that. He was a very gutsy actor, and you were never quite sure what he would do next. Sometimes he could be badly behaved, so they'd have to step in and put him in his place. He was a young man though at the time.

The director on *The Curse of the Werewolf* was Terence Fisher, who had directed Michael in four previous Gothic horror outings. Michael when speaking of Terence notes:

Oliver Reed as the doomed lead of *The Curse of the Werewolf* (Hammer, 1960) in his jail cell with the "old soak" portrayed by Michael Ripper.

> To be honest with you, I didn't really work with Terry a great deal. But he was always very quiet on the set, a very nice little chap, who knew exactly what he wanted. Terry's best work as a director was definitely those Gothic horrors. He used to say they were. They were definitely his baby.

Character actors were a main staple of Hammer Film Productions and along with Michael Ripper, actors such as George Woodbridge, Thorley Walters, Marne Maitland, George Pastell and Miles Malleson often appeared.

> Malleson was the funniest man I ever met. He could have you in stitches. He was an amazing comic, his delivery

The Curse of the Werewolf

in Eastman COLOR

CLIFFORD EVANS
OLIVER REED
YVONNE ROMAIN
CATHERINE FELLE

of lines and timing were first rate. Everyone at Hammer loved Miles because he was just so funny. He had one of those faces that fits comedy. No one could keep a straight face when Miles was around. I know dear old Christopher found it difficult to act with him because of this. He was a wonderful, truly great person.

It is true that Miles Malleson, like Michael, was a Hammer favorite, because he too would make the most of his often too-few lines. Their scenes were often short, but both were notorious scene stealers.

Miles Malleson had his own certain style often playing nice, rather bumbling characters. Terence Fisher once said of him:

Give Miles two lines and he'll work throughout the scene.

Something which Michael had done in film after film. Both actors had a certain knack of shining in their own way, and it was noticeable. In 1962 Michael appeared in the first of three swashbucklers for Hammer.

Christopher Lee is held at gunpoint by Mac (Michael Ripper) in the Hammer swashbuckler *The Pirates of Blood River* **(1962).**

The first was *The Pirates of Blood River* in which Michael was acting once again with his dear friend Christopher Lee.

> We had a God awful scene in that one. It was a location shoot in Black Park near Pinewood, by now a familiar haunt to Hammer Films. It was a swamp scene we were filming. Hell it was dreadful. Well this swamp was actually a lake, but Christ the stink, the smell from it was hideous. It was pollution at its worst, the water was just heavily stagnant. But the worst of it was me and about 20 other actors including Christopher Lee and Ollie Reed had to go into this lake from Hell. It was appalling, dreadful, I was most unhappy about this and so I think was Christopher. He was the first one to go in as he was the leader of our pirate band. When you got into this lake, as well as the smell you had underwater horrors to deal with, branches and suchlike. You literally sank into the

RANSACKING A LOST TROPIC ISLAND... FOR A FABULOUS IDOL OF GOLD!

The Pirates of Blood River

COLOR

KERWIN MATHEWS · GLENN CORBETT · CHRISTOPHER LEE · MARLA LANDI

thick mud that was under your feet. I must admit I was in fear of drowning. Dear old Christopher was almost up to his chin in it and he's a big chap. A very kind actor called Kerwin Mathews dragged his way with me through this horror and actually held onto me. Ollie Reed had a fight scene in the muck, and I got splashed in the face

Michael Ripper indulges in some nefarious pirating in *The Pirates of Blood River* (Hammer).

> quite heavily. Believe me I was glad to get back onto dry land, but it did leave one or two actors feeling quite ill, me included.

Sammy Davis, Jr. visited the set of *The Pirates of Blood River* during shooting. He was a self-confessed Hammer fan and close friend of both Christopher Lee and Peter Cushing. Michael recalls the day Sammy turned up on the set of the film:

> He seemed to be a nice, jokey kind of guy, genuinely interested in our films, the studio and all that was being shown. Christopher Lee, who I know was a close friend of Sammy's, enjoyed showing him around Bray that

"You literally sank into the thick mud that was under your feet," Michael Ripper remarked on this scene in *The Pirates of Blood River* (Hammer). Kerwin Mathews helps Ripper stay upright during filming.

day. But I didn't actually get to speak to him very much myself. We did exchange hellos though and I do actually remember him very kindly complimenting my work in Hammer films.

On his next swashbuckling adventure *The Scarlet Blade* Michael was under the direction of John Gilling. However, on day one Gilling would have a problem with Michael.

The thing is, I had just decided never again to ride a horse. A few months earlier on the set of *The Pirates of Blood River* I had witnessed actor Glenn Corbett, who was a well trained horseman, fall from his horse, sustain very serious injuries and so had to be hospitalized. So anyway, when John Gilling came to me and told me to get into the saddle, I refused. No matter how hard he tried to get me to mount, I wouldn't do it. I stood tall for once in my

life and they had no option but to hire a stunt man to take over from me for all horse riding scenes. I don't think John was too pleased about any of this. Anyway, after this, some clever close-ups of me were shot, showing me supposedly to be on a horse back, in action. Now after

In *Devil-Ship Pirates* (Hammer, 1964) Sir Basil (Ernest Clark) orders Pepe (Ripper) and Antonio (Charles Houston) be set free.

these were edited in no one could tell that it wasn't me. As a matter of fact, I was complimented for being by far the best horseman of the lot.

Appearing in *The Scarlet Blade* with Michael was Oliver Reed. Michael recalls an incident on the set of the film, involving Reed:

He was getting a bit carried away with one of the young ladies working on the film, and saying things he shouldn't. Well he brought me into this conversation and, in a way, I put my foot in it, stepped where you shouldn't with Ollie and told him that I didn't agree with what he was saying. So he got angry, threw his drink in my face and stormed off. Later that day he came to me with his dresser, and Ollie let his dresser throw a drink in his face in return. He then apologized to me for the earlier outburst and we shook hands. I was pleased it was over.

Ripper uses his expressive eyes in this scene with Natasha Pyne in *Devil-Ship Pirates* (Hammer).

In the third and last of Michael's swashbucklers for Hammer, *Devil-Ship Pirates*, something happened which could have turned into a very serious accident. Michael tells the story:

> It really was a miracle. There must have been at least 100 people on the set that day, actors and crew, and thankfully nobody was drowned. It was at Bray and we were in about 30 feet of water on board a full size replica of the ship *Diablo*. The vessel was once again the ingenious design of Bernard Robinson. On either side of this wonderful construction were drums, which were used as staging for the camera and lights. They had pumps to keep them dry and this day the director of the film, Don Sharp, insisted that the pumps be stopped. Just as they were stopped, the teaboat arrived, so everyone rushed to the teaboat side of the ship to get a refreshing drink and bite to eat, big mistake. With all on board on one side of the vessel, the

Martin Benson and Ripper as Jeremiah Mipps in *Captain Clegg* (U.S. Title: *Night Creatures*, Hammer, 1962).

Diablo capsized, toppling over on one side. Many people were thrown into the water. Even the camera, lighting, cables, all the electrical equipment went overboard. When I realized the ship was going I just rushed to the highest point of the vessel as quick as I could. I remember Christopher Lee, one other fellow and a girl were with me, holding on for dear life. In the water it was terrible panic, but luckily no one was seriously hurt. Believe me, though, if luck hadn't been present that day, many people would have been killed, including members of the cast. It certainly shook me and Christopher up.

Michael looks back at his time as a swashbuckling pirate:

Michael Ripper appeared with Peter Cushing for the first time in *Captain Clegg* (Hammer).

They were good films, but very difficult to make. Disaster was hidden around every corner, but we all came out the other end relatively unscathed. Me and Christopher shared quite a few jokes and laughs on those two Pirate films. Sadly though he wasn't in *The Scarlet Blade*. If I'm right in saying, *The Pirates of Blood River* was the 10th biggest international take at the box office in 1962.

In 1962 Michael played Jeremiah Mipps in Hammer's *Captain Clegg* and appeared for the first time in scenes with Peter Cushing. He said:

I had a good part in that opposite Peter. It was the only time we both worked together at Hammer. I didn't get to know him that well, he was a very quiet man, but like Christopher a brilliant actor, perfectionist and a very

Ripper as Tom meets Ray Barrett and Jennifer Daniel in *The Reptile* (Hammer, 1966), which featured one of Ripper's best roles at Hammer.

important part of Hammer films. I am sure without them both, the company would not have become as successful as it did.

Also appearing in *Captain Clegg* was actor Martin Benson. He said this about Michael:

I remember Michael as a true professional and a companionable colleague.

In his next two Gothic horrors for the company, *The Reptile* and *The Plague of the Zombies*, which were filmed back to back, Michael played two of his greatest roles for Hammer.

In *The Reptile* he played Innkeeper Tom Bailey, and in *The Plague of the Zombies* he played the role of Sergeant Swift.

Both are Gothic horror at their best, especially *The Plague of the Zombies*, which holds some very impressive scenes including a classic dream sequence of the dead rising from their graves. Michael is excellent in both playing two completely different characters. Tom Bailey the innkeeper in *The Reptile* is a very sympathetic and often funny character.

Ray Barrett and Michael Ripper search for an answer to the mystery of *The Reptile* (Hammer).

In one scene in which actor Ray Barrett enters his bar and empties locals for the second time, Michael delivers the line, "Well, you've emptied my pub again, haven't you? I think you'd better buy a drink for yourself before you bankrupt me."

In *The Plague of the Zombies*, Michael's character of Sergeant Swift is a bullying, much stronger character, giving Michael a chance for some serious acting.

Playing opposite Michael in *The Plague of the Zombies* was actor Brook Williams. He said:

> I would describe Michael Ripper as an easy going, good humored and good spirited person. *The Plague of the Zombies* was one of my first feature film parts , and Michael was very kind, generous and helpful to me when filming. Not long after the film had been released, I was doing another movie with Elizabeth Taylor and Richard Burton, and heard that their close friend Sammy Davis, Jr. would be visiting them on set. Well, I happened to be in the company of Elizabeth and Richard when Sammy ar-

The Reptile is a consistently enjoyable film and often overlooked by Hammer fans.

rived. To my surprise when he entered the room he totally ignored them and came rushing over to me, and pointing at me he said, *The Plague of the Zombies.* He continued by saying he was a big fan of Hammer films, and told me he had a collection of these movies at his home, with *The Plague of the Zombies* being a particular favorite. He then began reciting mine, Michael Ripper's and everyone else's dialogue in the movie. No, I'm not joking, he actually knew the dialogue word for word. I was quite surprised to discover that he was such a big fan. Now the last time I saw Michael Ripper was a few years ago. I was asked to appear on a television talk show about horror films etc., and was asked if I knew of anyone else who might like to be involved. Well, I instantly thought of Michael, and arranged for him to be chauffeur driven to and from the studio. Michael was very good on the show. He was

A portrait of Michael Ripper as Tom Bailey in *The Reptile* (Hammer).

Michael Ripper in a scene from *The Mummy's Shroud* (Hammer, 1966) with John Phillips.

modest, but very authoritative. Afterwards we were given a glass of champagne, and we sat talking about the old days, filming *The Plague of the Zombies*. I considered it nothing special, just another of Hammer's horror films. But today it's considered a classic. The dream sequence is a scene people remember the most from the movie, and if a clip from this film is shown on television, it is usually this one that is chosen. Sadly that film was the only time myself and Michael Ripper would work together.

Both *The Reptile* and *The Plague of the Zombies* were directed by John Gilling. Michael recalls:

Well John was certainly not the best director I ever worked with, but to be quite honest with you, he did always manage to bring out the best in me as an actor and I was always pleased with my performances under his direc-

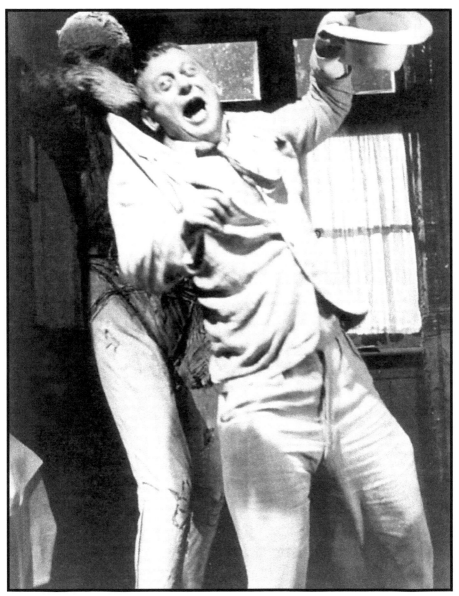

Longbarrow (Ripper) is attacked by the mummy in *The Mummy's Shroud* (Hammer).

tion. I thoroughly enjoyed working with him, although we would occasionally clash.

A year later Michael was back again with Gilling and, even though the film *The Mummy's Shroud* was not Hammer's best by a very long shot, it is certainly worth watching for Michael's memorable performance.

Ripper as the doomed Longbarrow in *The Mummy's Shroud* (Hammer).

I had a lovely part in that and it was the last thing I ever did for John Gilling. I played a poor down-trodden little

The intrepid explorers before they encounter the mummy in *The Mummy's Shroud* (Hammer).

P.R.O. twit called Longbarrow, who was dying to get back
to England, and who ended up being Mummy fodder.

The reviews for *The Mummy's Shroud* were largely of a scathing kind, although several did single out Michael's Longbarrow as a particularly fine character study. Playing the Mummy in *The Mummy's Shroud* was stunt performer and actor Eddie Powell. He said:

Michael Ripper was a lovely man to work with, and I do
remember one episode many years ago. I bumped into
Michael in the West End of London and of course chat-

ted about films, etc. and Michael said he was looking for work, or to coin a phrase he was resting. Since I was about to start work on a Hammer film, I suggested he get in touch with the company. He said he couldn't do that and decided he should contact his agent. I convinced him that since his agent hadn't been in touch, it was possible that he [the producer] was thinking of someone else for the film. I told him that the producer of the film, namely Tony Keys, a really wonderful man, could be approached direct, something I'd done myself in the past, and that Michael could do the same. After chatting further he finally agreed to do so and happily got the part. I've no idea after so many years and so many Hammer films that I've worked on, what the name of the film was.

In a previous Hammer mummy film, *The Curse of the Mummy's Tomb*, Michael's part of Achmed the Arab was so small if you blinked you would miss him. It was somewhat of a joke. He had no lines and sat for most of his 34 seconds of screen time in the background eating a sandwich. I don't know how he managed it, but once again he steals the scene. You begin to wonder why he was cast in such a pathetic little part. Was he put there for the regular Hammer cinema audience who had become used to his face turning up in all sorts of cameos? It is certainly his most unusual role for the company, but still a little gem in its own way. Michael said of his role in the film:

I don't think there was any joke behind it. To me it was just another role which I was happy to accept.

Hammer left Bray Studios in October 1966. Michael said:

The last film to be made at that studio was *The Mummy's Shroud*. When I finished my final day on that film I must admit I was upset. To leave Bray and that period of Hammer behind was a sad moment indeed. I knew I would miss it, well of course I would, I'd made over 20 films at that old building.

Michael looks back at his time at Bray:

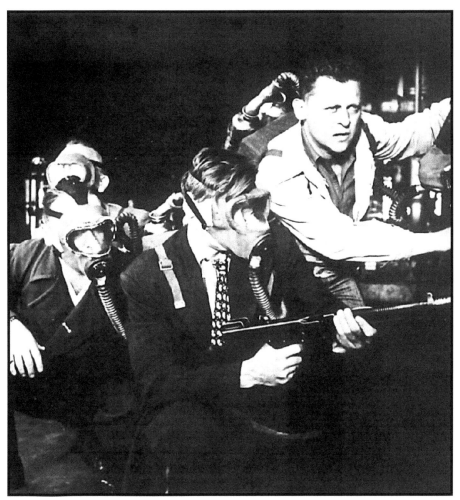

Although Ripper experienced cold and near drowning during his stint at Bray he remembers it as "a lovely place." Pictured: *Quatermass II* **(Hammer).**

It was great, absolutely great. My own opinion is that all the best Hammer Films were made there, especially out of the horrors. It was a fine studio, everything worked smoothly and even the food was good. It was a lovely place, a dream of a studio, most efficiently run. There were no other films going on there, except the one you were doing, which is a good thing. So this meant there were no distractions, like fighting for food in the canteen. The unity there was unique. Everyone was so involved. Most of all though it had a wonderful atmosphere.

Michael Ripper as Max in *Dracula Has Risen from the Grave* (Hammer, 1968).

Hammer moved to Pinewood and Elstree Film Studios, and yes, they took Michael Ripper with them. Michael went on to appear in three Dracula films for the company, with all three starring Christopher Lee as the cloaked count.

The first of these was *Dracula Has Risen from the Grave*, directed by Freddie Francis.

MOON ZERO TWO

JAMES OLSON · CATHERINA VON SCHELL
WARREN MITCHELL · ADRIENNE CORRI · ORI LEVY · DUDLEY FOSTER
and BERNARD BRESSLAW

A.B.C. GENERAL RELEASE OCTOBER 26!

Freddie was a good friend of mine. I did a number of films for him. I think he is a very good director. Like Terry Fisher he was very quiet on set, no fuss, no bother, just very efficient.

A science fiction film was the next Hammer film for Michael.

Moon Zero Two it was called. I don't think I've ever seen that film. I believe it was a terrible flop at the time. That's probably why I've never bothered to watch it. I know it got bad notices and nobody went to see it. Personally I couldn't understand that, as I thought it was a good script.

In his last horror film for Hammer, Michael was back playing an innkeeper again, or landlord, as he was called, in *Scars of Dracula*, which was filmed in May and June 1970. Michael said:

Michael Ripper as Cobb examines the body of Geoffrey Keen in *Taste the Blood of Dracula* **(Hammer, 1969).**

I had a dramatic role in that, a pretty good part.

Michael played briefly in the film with actor Patrick Troughton.

I liked Pat. A really lovely chap. In the film he plays a kind of henchman to Dracula. He had terrible nerves Pat. Used to shake bad. Fabulous actor though.

Playing Dracula once again was Christopher Lee. Michael said:

I must be the only person in the world who can say they shared a joke with Dracula. Dear old Christopher, he used to stride about in that long black cape looking very sinister indeed.

By this time Hammer was adding sex to films to keep audiences' attention:

I don't know whether sex was actually necessary or not in Hammer films. It was without a doubt one of the best

Michael Ripper (back to camera on right) in a scene from *Scars of Dracula* **(Hammer, 1970) with Jenny Hanley and Dennis Waterman (third left).**

ways to get people into the cinema, and I suppose still is.
If you have a bit of sex you're going to draw more people
than if you don't.

Because of his appearance in several Dracula films, Michael once
was asked if he did actually believe in such things as vampirism. He
would respond:

I don't really know. I think most things are possible
as far as the human race is concerned. I've met some
pretty vampiric people, whether they drink blood or not,

Ripper as Cobb with Anthony Corlan in *Taste the Blood of Dracula* (Hammer).

> I couldn't say. Where mankind is concerned, I don't think anything is too fantastic.

It was in the early 1970s that Michael, like Peter Cushing and Christopher Lee, started being tagged as something of a horror actor. He said:

> It's better to be known as a horror actor than not to be known at all. An actor is earning his living, the same as anybody else. Very often a man is forced to take a job that he doesn't particularly like. If it pays, you take it. Fortunately in this business you are often offered something that you do like.

Michael's close friend Anthony Hinds had been with Hammer since Michael had joined the company in 1947. However, in 1970, Hinds left Hammer and only returned to the profession to write the odd screenplay under his pen name John Elder.

Michael recalls his association with Anthony Hinds:

Tony Hinds was absolutely great. He made Hammer what it became. It's strange really because we were always in touch with each other and then when we left Hammer he ceased having anything to do with me. Plus, I think I'm right in saying that I was only one of many people that he never had anything to do with after that. I do think he was unhappy with how Hammer was changing in the late 1960s. Tony was such a good friend of mine and a neighbor when I lived in the country out in Oxfordshire. But it did upset me a great deal when I couldn't contact him, because he'd moved out of the country. Why I became out of touch with Tony, I just don't know. But there must have been some very good reason. I don't think it had anything to do with me. I think he just wanted to forget Hammer and all who were connected with it. You see, to me Tony Hinds was Hammer, he was it, and he left because he said he was unhappy. But personally I think he ended up being bought out of it. Very sad, and I think perhaps the reason he didn't keep in contact. After he left I never really worked for the company again myself. I think I actually made one more film for them, a comedy. But I think the reason why I never seemed to be employed by the company again had something to do with my friendship with Tony. I might be wrong about that, but it's the only way I can make any sense of it. Tony was a creative man, and he created a channel, that actors like me, we could feel the channel. When he left it was sad. Poor old Tony.

Michael's final performance in a Hammer film came in 1971 in a comedy about funeral directors called *That's Your Funeral*. Michael played the small role of Arthur, a railway man with a strong north-of-England dialect. Appearing with him in the film were Raymond Huntley and Bill Fraser. Michael said:

Raymond I'd worked with several times. A great comic actor. So was Bill Fraser. It was a good scene we had together in that film. All three of us had to speak very northern.

Hammer would go on to make several more horror and comedy films, but Michael would never work for the company again. Not even as part of their television series *Hammer House of Horror*. It was definitely Hammer's loss.

Michael was once asked what he liked most about the company.

The fact that they employed me.

Small Screen

In 1961 Michael's sister Barbara died. He said:

> We had always been very close, and kept in constant touch
> with each other. She was a great loss to me, and I still
> miss her dearly.

During the 1960s other than almost continuous work with Hammer, Michael did have time to appear in other films for other companies. These included the classic war films *Sink the Bismarck* in which Michael was working with director Lewis Gilbert for the fourth time, and *The Spy Who Came in from the Cold* in which Michael appeared as Lofthouse. But like *Sink the Bismarck* before it, Michael's part was uncredited.

It is difficult to believe that an actor of Michael's standing could go totally uncredited although the parts he plays in both films are brief—he only appears for a few seconds and has hardly any lines. But this is no excuse for uncrediting a fine character actor who adds weight to all the scenes he appears in. Hammer Film Productions would never have done such a thing.

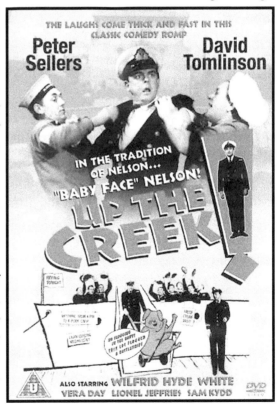

Often Michael was wasted in pathetic bit parts which were unworthy of his talent. Four such films are *The Naked Truth*, *Up the Creek*, *Further Up the Creek* and *Bobbikins*. All four films could have made better use of Michael.

Ripper (left) with Eric Barker (center) and Thorley Walters in the continuing St. Trinian's series: *The Pure Hell of St. Trinian's* **(British Lion, 1960).**

The film *The Pure Hell of St. Trinian's*, the third in the series, saw Michael return once again as Eric, the liftman. This time Michael played opposite actors Thorley Walters and Dennis Price. This film is especially fun for Ripper fans because of a wonderful credit sequence where he does a bit of dancing.

In *A Prize of Arms* Michael's role was small, but he got a chance to appear with a top British star of the 1950s and 1960s, Stanley Baker. Michael said:

> Stanley was one of the friendliest men you could work with.

In the 1960s Michael would appear in several films which would become his own personal favorites. *Every Day's a Holiday* was one. "I loved that film," Michael said. This was followed by *Where the Bullets Fly* in which Michael played Angel. "I enjoyed my role in that. It would have been a fabulous part if it had been a big, expensive picture. But it wasn't. Well what do you expect, I was in it."

In *Torture Garden*, directed by Freddie Francis for Amicus Productions, Michael played Gordon Roberts and worked opposite

two of America's big stars, Burgess Meredith and Jack Palance. Michael remembers:

> Palance didn't really have much to do with me. He was easy to work with though, and always friendly. Meredith was a great person, very amusing, we got on really well. Both actors were quite big business over in America. I know Meredith had just finished playing the Penguin in the popular *Batman* series. I know that because he told us lots of stories, he was a great storyteller. But he, like Palance, was not big-headed, they were just very nice people. Freddie Francis was director, and I actually think it was the first time we worked together. I thought the idea of four separate stories in one film was quite good. Oh

Michael Ripper with his second wife Catherine Finn in the garden at Larkrise in Chinnor, Oxfordshire in 1962.

yes, and I remember I had to stab Meredith to death with a pair of scissors at the end of that film. It was all a trick though, set up to frighten some people. I had a good part.

Looking back, Michael reminisces about four film performers he bumped into regularly on his trips in and out of different film studios.

Sidney James was a frequenter of the bar at Pinewood Studios, and you would always know if Sid was in there

Michael Ripper with his daughter Susan at Larkrise in 1962.

entertaining because you would hear that unmistakable laugh. He was one of the most down to earth people you could meet, and he got on well with anyone and everyone. He'd buy you a drink and entertain you with different stories. Sid was a lover of horse-racing and liked to put on a bet. The first time I met him was on a film called *The Rainbow Jacket*, but I don't think we actually appeared together in that film, but to be honest, I'm not sure about that. Peter Sellers was another great comedy actor I bumped into a few times. Now I had heard he could be a difficult man. But whenever I came across him he was always cheerful and always spoke, even if it was just hello. Margaret Rutherford was wonderful. She was wildly eccentric and very comical. She used to drive behind the wheel of a Morris Minor car, and was very whimsical, quaint, an absolute delight to meet. Sadly we never worked together. Frankie Howerd was in the last of the St. Trinian's films. We didn't appear together, but I did get to meet him. When you saw him at work, either on TV or film, he always came over as being a very confident man. But to meet him he was totally opposite. He was a terribly shy man and always looked somewhat sad. Having said this, Frankie was always approachable, he liked to meet and talk to people, even though he would give the impression that he didn't by hiding away in corners. Frankie lacked confidence like many of us actors. He liked to talk to you, and was always a patient listener and seemed very interested in what yu had to say. He was a joy to sit and chat with.

Patrick McGoohan in *Dangerman*

Michael moved from his home in Chinnor, Oxfordshire in 1970, and took up residence in a new house in Emsworth, Hampshire. This new home was very close to where his daughter Susan and brother Peter live. Catherine Finn was still with Michael and joined him at the new place in Emsworth. They had been together for 23 years, but were still not a married couple. In 1971 when Michael's work suddenly dried up for Hammer Films he turned to television, and this is where he would remain. From now on he would

1963 portrait of Michael Ripper.

only make an occasional appearance in a feature film and would on one instance make a return to the theatre.

During the 1960s Michael made appearances in several classic television productions— *Dangerman* with Patrick McGoohan, *Maigret* with Rupert Davies and *The Saint* with Roger Moore, etc. *The Saint* would be the second time Michael had worked with the suave Roger Moore.

Previously he had worked with him in the 1950s series *Ivanhoe*. Michael remembered Roger, and some of the TV he did in the 1960s:

> Roger was always fun to work with. His delivery of lines was a dream to witness, a very dry delivery. Freddie Francis directed that *Saint* episode. Some of the TV I did was pretty much rubbish, because the programs were made very cheaply, and had flimsy sets. I never watched if I thought they were bad because I do think your performance suffered. I won't begin to name shows I thought were bad, but there was plenty made, and yes, I appeared in most of them. It's funny because one program I worked on, a police series I think, but I'm not so sure. Anyway it was a ghastly, horrible thing, and the set was falling apart around the actors because it was so cheaply made, and then it caught fire. The director and crew were rushing around with fire extinguishers trying to put out the flames. But I remember much of the set was destroyed. I cannot for the life of me recall which series it was that I was appearing in. Wouldn't tell you though, if I could. Lots of shows I did were good, like *The Saint* and *Dangerman*, simply because care was taken when making them and they were made with slightly more money, which helped. Basically they were a lot more expensive looking.

In the early 1970s Michael was not happy with his decline in the film world. He said:

> I enjoyed films much more than television, and did get pretty sad when the film offers stopped coming in as frequently. However the money was always good on television, much better than film, and you always seemed to be offered better parts. But my first love was films. Theatre was a big favorite but that was all cocked up after the throat operation.

In 1966 Michael played the character Eric, the liftman for the final time in the last of the St. Trinian's comedy films *The Great St. Trinians Train Robbery*. The film, directed by Frank Launder, had an all-star cast in-

cluding Frankie Howerd, Dora Bryan, George Cole, Reg Varney, Richard Wattis, Raymond Huntley, Arthur Mullard and Norman Mitchell. Mitchell has been a friend of Michael's for many years and remembers it was Michael who got him his part in the above film:

> An actor had fallen out of the film, and it was Michael's recommendation to his friend, the director Frank Launder, that persuaded him to cast me in the part of the toastmaster. Which was a very good role. So I am very grateful to Michael.

Michael had no scenes with Mitchell in the final film. He appears with Richard Wattis and Raymond Huntley. He said:

> Yes I was with Raymond once again. But all of my scenes were with Richard Wattis, a very funny fellow and we had a lot of laughs. It's a shame the St. Trinian's films didn't continue. But perhaps they had run out of steam and were considered to be a bit out of date. I don't know to be honest. But I do think Launder and Gilliat would like to have continued, as they both actually told me this on various occasions I spent with them chatting at their homes.

It was in 1972, after 25 years together, that Michael and Catherine Finn finally tied the knot. The marriage ceremony, like Michael's first, was a small affair.

1972 also saw Michael and Catherine appear for the first time in a film together. It was a Gothic horror, *The Creeping Flesh,* directed by Freddie Francis and starring Peter Cushing and Christopher Lee in the lead roles. Michael's role in the film is that of Carter, who helps Peter Cushing into his home with a skeleton of a primitive man which has been discovered in New Guinea. Even though Michael's part is basically a fun little cameo, he is wasted once again. His mere cough and a spit part are over far too soon. Ripper fans wish his scene with Peter Cushing had lasted much longer. Actor George Benson plays Peter's assistant in the film, a character who could have easily been played by Michael.

Many people knew of Michael's abilities and qualities as an actor. It remains a mystery why studios didn't take the opportunity to cast him in larger roles. It would have been wonderful if Michael had played the bumbling George Benson part in *The Creeping Flesh*. Catherine Finn fares much better in the film, playing the part of Emily, maid to Peter Cushing.

Away from work, Michael for many years had been a sailing man and had owned and sailed boats. While living in Emsworth, he used to travel regularly to Poole Harbour in Dorset, about 50 miles from his home. It was here that Michael kept his own 30-foot sailing boat, which he had named *White Witch*. It was very much a relaxing thing for him. He said:

> I used to love to put on the old sailing cap and go out to sea.
> Marvelous, nothing better for relaxing and keeping your
> mind away from other things. I had one or two different
> boats, but the one at Poole Harbour was my favorite.

Apart from the boats Michael had other enjoyable pastimes which included music, photography and brewing his own beer and making wine.

> Oh yes, there has got to be more to life than just acting.
> I mean when I was living in Oxfordshire I liked to look
> after the garden and orchard. When I was in Emsworth it
> was more the boat. But I had always had a love of music,

photography; I owned some pretty good photographic cameras. Plus I liked to barrel my own beers and make my own wines. Very bloody strong though, no drinking and driving or sailing after that. I must admit that I have been lucky sometimes in my life to be able to afford wonderful things. To be able to build my own house, to own boats. But really if it wasn't for the acting work I wouldn't really have been able to enjoy many of these things.

Because of filming engagements in London and elsewhere, Michael was getting tired of traveling the great distance from his home in Emsworth to the capital. So in 1972 he decided to put his house on the market. But in doing so he hit upon a bit of very bad luck. Michael takes up the story:

> I sold my house in Emsworth and got what I thought was a good price for it. But very quickly after that houses went up a lot in price. So I was never in a position then to buy a place worth having. I had sold my house for what turned out to be nothing. So I was very unlucky.

In an attempt to find more money in order to get himself a decent place in London, Michael sold his boat at Poole Harbour, and sadly, would never get the chance to buy another and set sail again. Michael eventually found himself a small terraced house on a street in Islington, north London, and it is in Islington where he still lives today.

Blink and you miss his bit part as the traffic warden with Beryl Reid in the film farce *No Sex Please, We're British*. This film followed after his move to London. In some television versions of this movie, Michael's

Michael Ripper as Cedric with Alan Curtis in *Sir Yellow* (Yorkshire Television, 1973). The costumes were designed by Michael's future wife, Cecelia Doidge-Ripper.

scenes have been totally cut out. It is actually a nice little cameo, be it very small. In fact, it's worth seeing for Michael stalling Reid's Morris Minor car and driving it away to a more suitable place other than double yellow lines. He no sooner drives out of shot when Reid delivers the classic line, "Little Hitler."

Sir Yellow (**Yorkshire Television**) **with Bob Hoskins, Arthur Mullard, Alan Curtis and Michael Ripper.**

The 1970s, like the 1950s and 1960s, saw Michael once again in great demand as an actor on television. *Sir Yellow* filmed in 1973 at Yorkshire Television studios in Leeds gave Michael a good villainous role in a six-part situation medieval comedy series. Jimmy Edwards played the lead with Melvyn Hayes, Alan Curtis and Arthur Mullard playing good supporting roles. Even Bob Hoskins turned up in it. Actor Alan Curtis played opposite Michael in the series. He recalled:

> Michael was by far the most experienced film and television actor out of myself, Jimmy Edwards, Melvyn Hayes and Arthur Mullard. He was easy to work with, very professional, and as an actor he had an extensive range of very funny facial expressions. Michael also never caused a fuss like most actors if changes were made to the script at the last minute, as he had been used to live television where you had to learn the lines quick and just do it. Rehearsals for *Sir Yellow* were enormous fun as we all enjoyed ad-libbing, but most especially Jimmy Edwards who was a

master at this and had us all in hysterics with his antics. Michael and I both had a love of music, and near to the Yorkshire Television Studios in Leeds was a great record shop which we both visited regularly and enjoyed buying records. The summer of '73 when we filmed *Sir Yellow*, was very nice and warm and me and Michael both enjoyed getting away from London for a short while to stay and film in and around Leeds. Sadly the series itself wasn't very successful. We rehearsed for a second series but it was dropped before filming began. Sadly it was the only time I would work with Michael.

From Yorkshire Television Michael jumped to Thames Television were he appeared in the popular children's television series, *The Adventures of Black Beauty*.

In fact Michael successfully moved from one TV company to another, and worked for most if not all of the main ones. Along the way he worked for Thames Television, Yorkshire Television, London Weekend Television, BBC Television, Anglia Television, Southern Television, A.T.V. and Central Television. Quite a list and a big achievement on its own. Few actors are able to do this and Michael was most certainly on that short list of talent who could accomplish this feat.

Tyburn Productions cast Michael as Sewerman in their film *Legend of the Werewolf* in 1974. It's a memorable part but once again I am sure more could have been made of it for Michael's sake. At least when you consider that the screenplay was written by Michael's old friend

Anthony Hinds, writing under his pen name John Elder. Michael appears for less than two minutes in the film and has no lines or dialogue. In the film Michael plays an old tramp down in the sewers fishing for cigarette ends so he can fill his pipe with the unused tobacco. Along comes the Werewolf played by newcomer David Rintoul, and makes a meal of the old tramp's throat. Another Michael Ripper character which we are not given enough time to get to know. This lovable little tramp created by Michael Ripper, who made the most of his screen time, could have surely been developed more as a character on paper. But let us be thankful that he was cast at all—even though he is onscreen for less than two minutes, it's worth the wait.

Another big television company Michael worked with on several occasions was Granada TV in Manchester. He had first worked for the

Crown Court featured numerous guest stars, inclduing Michael Ripper.

company in 1961 appearing in their series, *Knight Errant*. All we know about this lost television performance is that Michael played a character called Black Knight.

In the 1970s Michael appeared in several different series for Granada including *Crown Court* and definitely the most famous program to come out of the studios, *Coronation Street*.

Michael recalls his appearance in this long running British soap opera:

> I played a drunk but was only in one episode and spent most of that locked in the toilets of the Rovers Return Inn. I met some of the people who played unforgettable characters in *The Street*. Jean Alexander who played Hilda Ogden, Violet Carson who played Ena Sharples and Pat Phoenix who played Elsie Tanner. It was nice to play a small part in what was and still is a very popular program.

In 1975 Michael appeared in an episode of the often violent police series about the Flying Squad called *The Sweeney*. Michael played Herbie Mew, a friend of the leading character, Detective Inspector Jack Regan, played by actor John Thaw. In the episode Michael's character Herbie gets mixed up with some crooks and ill-gotten money and Inspector Regan steps in to sort it out and set matters right. John Thaw, star of the series, had this to say:

I'm afraid I have no stories to tell about working with Michael on *The Sweeney*. As Michael will tell you, working on those programs was very intense! Suffice it to say that I have always been a great admirer of Michael's work and consider him to be one of our finest character actors.

It wouldn't be the last time Michael would work with Thaw. In 1987 Michael appeared in the Yorkshire Television comedy series *Home to Roost* in which Thaw played the leading role.

In 1976 Michael and Terence Fisher were guests at a horror convention being held over a weekend in London. A young lady, Brenda Marshall attended this show. She remembers:

Michael was really lovely with everyone, chatting and laughing. I had my photograph taken with him which I now have framed on my wall at home. Like many others, I am a big fan of his work. I enjoyed that convention very much, also I met Terence Fisher. It was an enormous pleasure to meet them both. I do hope I get the chance to meet Michael again someday. But if not, I wish him all the best for the future.

Budapest was the location for Michael's next film appearance, playing Raquel Welch's servant in Richard Fleischer's film, *The Prince and the Pauper*. The film boasted an all-star cast including George C. Scott, Charlton Heston, Ernest Borgnine, Rex Harrison and Harry Andrews. A great cast but Michael worked with none of them. He did however have the pleasure of working with Raquel Welch, and someone he hadn't seen for years, Oliver Reed. One evening, after filming, Michael with his dear friend Norman Mitchell (who was also appearing in the movie) went for a meal and drinks with Oliver.

Michael Ripper

Budapest is multi-Romantica, the bars have great string orchestras, Gypsy bands, marvelous red wine and great food. Nothing could have been better for the trio of Ripper, Mitchell and Reed. Everything was going well, lots of jokes and laughs, when suddenly Oliver said, "Let's have a food fight," and started throwing his food around. Michael and Norman got under the table, and somehow managed to make a quick exit into another bar. Meanwhile Oliver was arrested and put in jail. Michael remembers working with Raquel Welch:

> She was very bossy with me, but only in a jokey way.
> We got on fine.

Working in Budapest was strange for Michael since it was a very strict country at this time. Michael would go into a crowded bar with other actors laughing and joking and two police would arrive and there would be complete silence. Everyone would shut up in case they said something politically incorrect and be put in jail. Michael was glad to get back to England.

The late 1970s saw Michael appear in several comedy series. Three of these were highly popular at the time. *George and Mildred* with Brian Murphy and Yootha Joyce, *Sykes* with Eric Sykes and Hattie Jacques and *The Two Ronnies* with Ronnie Barker and Ronnie Corbett. The latter gave Michael a couple of occasions to show off his comedic talents in an enormously popular TV comedy series watched and loved by many people. In one of the shows, Michael played a comical Taxi Driver. Actor Ronnie Barker, now retired from show business and one of the stars of *The Two Ronnies*, had this to say about Michael:

> I remember Michael as a bright, cheerful and intelligent
> man, who was an extremely good character actor.

Thomas the Chauffeur in the hit BBC comedy series *Butterflies* would become Michael's best-remembered TV role. He said:

> That show gave me recognition I had not previously
> known. The thing is, whenever that series was being
> shown, I would be stopped in the street by people when-
> ever I ventured out of my house. I'm not complaining,
> it was very nice. Some would stop me because they in-

stantly knew I was in the series, and others would stop me thinking I was an old friend, but of course I wasn't, they had seen me in *Butterflies*. People were very friendly, it was all good fun.

When Michael first started work on the series in 1978, he hit a slight problem in his contract. The trouble was his fee for appearing in the program was hardly better than what he had received from the BBC nearly 20 years earlier. So in a fit of anger Michael got on the phone to his agent who then contacted the BBC in a bid to try to up Michael's ludicrously low contract fee. After much negotiation Michael and his agent managed to squeeze an extra £5 out of BBC Television.

Acting opposite Michael in *Butterflies* was actor Bruce Montague who played one of the main characters. Bruce looks back at his time working with Michael:

The series ran over a five-year period. Michael wasn't in the first few episodes. But my character—Leonard—had no way of communicating his feelings privately regarding Ria (played by Wendy Craig). So Carla Lane, writer on the series, introduced the chauffeur character Thomas, played by Michael, so I had someone to chat with. The old syndrome of thrillers—the Detective Sergeant or Inspector always having to have the Detective Constable so as to have someone in which to confide. Michael was a delight to work with, and we got on terribly well as friends. He used to tell me stories of his early days in the film industry as an assistant director. When we worked together we had a great rapport. We were two old pros,

Wendy Craig and Bruce Montague in *Butterflies*

who learned our lines and got on with it. Most of the time shooting scenes in just one take, and Michael was always word perfect.

Bruce Montague at this time also became a regular visitor to Michael's home in Islington, North London. Bruce recalls:

> Michael had the most comprehensive music library I have ever seen. It must have rivaled the BBC's. He used to make his own beer and have a stack of barrels at home, with the strongest beer kept in the bottom barrel. I remember on my first visit to Michael's I started at the top barrel which wasn't very strong and slowly worked my way down. When I reached the bottom one Michael advised me against drinking it. Anyway he eventually got me a Sherry glass and poured me a bit in. I thought it wasn't strong, but then I tried to stand up and couldn't. It blew your head off.

Butterflies became Michael's first regular part on television, and the series itself was very popular with viewers.

Worzel Gummidge at the Repertory Theatre in Birmingham, 1980: Norman Mitchell, Mary Grifiths, Susan Jane Tannor, Lloyd McGuire, Jane Freeman, Michael Ripper and Graham Padden. (Courtesy Willoughby Gullachsen)

1978 saw Michael's second marriage to Catherine Finn end in divorce. They had been together for 31 years, but only married for six. However, before the marriage had even started it was on the rocks. Michael and Catherine decided it would be best to live apart. A divorce was settled not long after.

In addition to his character of Thomas in *Butterflies*, Michael played one other character regularly on television—grumpy old Mr. Shepherd in Southern Television's popular children's series, *Worzel Gummidge*. This was a series about a walking, talking scarecrow which gets up to all sorts of mischievous antics with friends John and Sue, Aunt Sally, an animated fairground doll and Worzel's creator, The Crowman. The series was a hit with adults and children alike since it was both funny and sad. In fact, *Worzel* was one of television's most successful creations and actor Jon Pertwee, who played the role brilliantly, considered it his best and made the part very much his own. Michael's character Mr. Shepherd, who

Michael Ripper as Mr. Shepherd with Jane Freeman and Jon Pertwee in *Worzel Gummidge* **at the Repertory Theatre, 1980. (Courtesy Willoughby Gullachsen)**

owns the doll Aunt Sally, is always fun to watch and is given plenty to do. The character created by Michael is serious, but on many occasions makes a fool of himself. In one episode Michael is given a chance to sail a boat again, but this time with mischievous Worzel and Aunt Sally on board. Michael recalls his time on the series:

> It was a fun, lovely, charming little series. Jon Pertwee was a great laugh. On one episode I gave him a few lessons on how to handle a boat. We had a great cast, which included my old friend Norman Mitchell. I also got along very well with Joan Sims, who played a snobbish character. Every episode was directed by James Hill, and I remember that the atmosphere on the series was very relaxed and all the cast got on well.

The series was mostly filmed on location at Kings Somborne and Braishfield in Hampshire. Braishfield was a little village where Michael's character, Mr. Shepherd, lived in a little cottage. Because of the success

Michael Ripper with Norman Mitchell in *Worzel Gummidge* at the Repertory Theatre, 1980. (Courtesy Willoughby Gullachsen)

of the series it was turned into a musical stage version. It had mostly the same cast including Jon Pertwee and Norman Mitchell and opened at Birmingham Repertory Theatre, Christmas 1980. However, Michael was not as happy in the stage show as he had been in the series. He said:

> As much as I love the theatre and in a way it was nice to be back, I had terrible trouble with my voice. In the theatre you have to have great voice projection and, even with the use of microphones, my voice just wasn't working properly. So sadly I felt I had to turn down future *Worzel* Christmas shows.

The show continued at Christmas for the next three years, going to the Cambridge Theatre in London, then to Southampton and back to Wimbledon, London. Sadly, Michael was not with the show, his part was taken by actor Frank Marlborough. Norman Mitchell who played the character P.C. Parsons in *Worzel* had his own memories of knowing and working with Michael:

We were both in four series of *Worzel Gummidge* and the stage version in Birmingham where we shared the same dressing room. When we first started on the series, Jon Pertwee said to me and Michael that "Worzel will be his and our old age pension." At Birmingham me and Michael used to meet every morning and have quiet drink in the nearest pub. We used to enjoy a glass of Guinness together. Michael always had top of the range cars and drove very well and very fast, a sort of Stirling Moss of *Worzel Gummidge*. He is a great artist. Always dead letter perfect, you never got a bum cue from Michael. He's very quiet, but got a great sense of humor. Lovely person. He used to make his own beer, very, very strong. After drinking it you'd think you were taking one step but were actually taking four.

Another actor who remembers Michael is Geoffrey Bayldon who played The Crowman in *Worzel Gummidge*. He said:

First of all, Michael and I sadly never had any scenes together in the series of *Worzel* or in the stage show. But Michael was a lovely man, we got on marvelously. He was always spotless, fun, warm, never dreary in any way. Loved his work and the people he worked with. He also had a great love of music.

After the final series of *Worzel* had finished filming, Michael found himself once again making appearances in famous British television programs. These included *Tales of the Unexpected*, *Lady Killers*, *Minder*, *The Pickwick Papers* and *The Baker Street Boys*, a BBC children's television series in which Michael played the character Stanley Fluff.

Crude, earthy, violent, hard hitting and brutally funny were used to describe the next film Michael appeared in—a tough black comedy called *No Surrender*. Actor James Ellis appeared alongside his friend Michael. James recalls his first day on the film:

In *No Surrender* the part of my sidekick and sparring partner (name of Napoleon [or Tony Bonaparte]) had not been decided upon, and naturally I was a bit anxious to

Michael Ripper as Tony Bonaparte with James Ellis in *No Surrender* (Film Four, 1985).

learn who it might be, since we had to function as a double act. Alan Bleasdale, the writer of the screenplay, insisted on buying me a drink and positioning me on a seat with a view of the entrance hall of the Adelphi Hotel in Liverpool. I remember thinking he was behaving a bit oddly, when suddenly Michael appeared in the doorway accompanied by the director of the film, Peter Smith. Newly arrived from the London train, Michael looked around a bit bewildered. Then we spotted each other and both our faces did light up. "That's our Napoleon," whispered Bleasdale in my ear as I ran to greet Michael. When Peter Smith and Alan saw our immediate rapport, they were obviously thrilled to bits. As the film progressed we dovetailed into every scene and had an absolutely marvelous time. That was another side of Michael's brilliance — a Stan Laurel flair for comedy and pathos, and total believable humanity. Michael has certainly had a most interesting and varied career and is much loved and respected by his colleagues in the business, and, of course, by a large film and theatre-going public and countless television viewers. I for one am a fan, as well as being a good friend.

No Surrender is certainly different from any of Michael's previous outings. The film is set in a seedy nightclub in Liverpool on New Year's Eve. A group of people turn up for a party, some in fancy dress including Michael, dressed in a Napoleon costume. Total mayhem ensues. Murder, fistfights, bottle fights and strong language are just part of the menu. This Film Four movie is something of a cult classic today and does have a small following of admirers. Michael and James are a delight to watch and work excellently together. Michael is fun in the movie, but also serious in certain scenes and slightly sinister. In one scene Michael breaks a bottle over the head of actor Ray McAnally and then kicks him repeatedly while he's down on the ground. It's really quite interesting to see Michael playing the inflicter of violence for once, rather than being the victim.

After this film Michael was back to working in television. One of his roles was in the series *In Sickness and in Health*, playing a man in an invalid chair at a football ground with Warren Mitchell as the infamous Alf Garnett.

In 1990 Michael appeared as a Porter in a number of episodes of *Jeeves and Wooster* with Stephen Fry and Hugh Laurie.

1991 saw Michael play an aging fisherman in the comedy horror film *Revenge of Billy the Kid*. Unfortunately, the film is not a classic and nowhere near the standard of any of Michael's ear-

Hugh Laurie and Stephen Fry in *Jeeves and Wooster*

A caricature of Michael Ripper by Paul Pickford, 1998.

lier films. Despite the often crude, vulgar and sick humor, there are one or two quite funny moments and some notable performances, one from Michael Balfour, Michael's old friend, playing an extremely vulgar old farmer. Norman Mitchell, another friend of Michael's, turns up in the smallest of bit parts, and Michael himself appears for a split second, but still manages to steal the scene. The film though is certainly not for the squeamish or easily offended.

For four years after this Michael didn't work as an actor at all, and when he did return to appear in an episode of *The Bill* he had to leave because of illness. However, another role was offered him in the series a few months later, which he was happy to accept.

In 1995 Michael appeared in what could be his last proper acting performance; however, his part in the popular soap opera *Eastenders* was so tiny it was hardly worth the great character actor turning out to the studio. Let us sincerely hope that this will not be the last ever Ripper performance.

But we shall have to wait and see, as only time will tell.

God Be With the Days

Today, Michael lives a quiet, relaxing life at his home in Islington, London, basically retired and happy to be out of the spotlight. He said:

> I'm glad really to be more or less out of the profession. The acting business is all about money today, and greed. Acting talent, I'm afraid, seems to take second place. In my day you did the job because you loved it. Not because you were paid well, because you never were.

Michael is one of the most modest, unassuming, nicest, kindest, gentlemanly actors you could ever meet, and does not consider himself special. In fact, he is totally unlike most actors. The cut-throat, back-stabbing, tough world of show business has not affected him at all. Michael, and many other actors of his generation, all seem to share this quality — unlike many of today's young actors who seem endlessly selfish.

Michael's personality is very much like that of the late Peter Cushing. Michael, like Peter, is a gentle man and always a gentleman. Today Michael is in physically great shape and hasn't really changed a great deal in 30 years, aside from being a little bit frailer — which is only natural for a man in his 80s. Michael still retains all those wonderful Ripper trademarks from his films — the big, bulging expressive eyes, the cheeky grin and that marvelous sense of humor.

However, there is also a serious side to Michael and when you find yourself in a conversation with him, it is fascinating. When he first spoke openly about his father, the actor in Michael, which very rarely appears, raised its head. For a split second he became his father, creating his voice and facial appearance. Michael is still haunted by the memories of those traumatic years with his father. Does Michael consider his life a happy one? He said:

Michael Ripper and Cecelia Doidge-Ripper on their wedding day at Walton-on-Thames in London, October 1995.

I have had a lot of happiness in my life. But I think my
life has been dominated by sadness and other things of that
nature. My father, for one, plays a big part in the sadness
of my life, and my worst memories are about him.

Michael's childhood and memories of his father are never totally
forgotten. He may have had a wonderful career in films and theatre, but
behind those comical characters are painful memories. When asked if
he is still affected by memories from his childhood he responded, "In
a way, yes I am."

It is important to point out here that this biography has not intended
to destroy the character of Harold Ripper. These are Michael's own
personal words and feelings about his father. However, this opinion of
Harold Ripper is not necessarily held by any other member of the Ripper family.

It is always a great pleasure to listen when Michael speaks about his
career as an actor, and after such conversations Michael will always end
by saying, "God Be With the Days."

Michael actually likes to watch his own films. To be able to sit with
and watch Michael viewing himself is a delight. In a way, it's also strange,
because he'll position himself right in front of the television set, put on
his glasses and laugh along with you as if he's watching someone else.
He also watches the films as if seeing them for the very first time, and
he always seems to enjoy them.

When asked if he enjoyed seeing himself on the screen he said:

I like to see what I'm up to on the screen. If you mean do
I get a thrill out of seeing myself, I would say probably
no. Occasionally I may think, "Christ Mike, you were
good there." But that very rarely happens. But I think
I'm all right. I did the best I could.

This leads onto another question. How did he manage to play such
a wide variety of characters and create so many different facial appearances? Did he think about how he could play the characters? Did he base
his characters on anyone?

No, I never thought about how I could play the character, I just played it. I also never based my characters on anyone. I'm not one of those people who sits on a bus and says, I'll play it like him. I play them more like me. In acting, as in life, it's no good trying to be like someone else. It's a waste of time. You should create your own style. There is definitely no method to my acting.

Michael has appeared in many modern and period pictures. He was once asked which he preferred:

I don't mind either way really. It's just the same with me putting on a suit and tie as me putting on tights.

It is sad that the name Michael Ripper will mean nothing to many of today's cinema-going public. But it is his face that many people remember. Often when you mention the name Michael Ripper to people, they would respond, "Who's he?" But, if you were to produce a photograph of the dear man from your pocket, "Oh yes, I know him all right," they would reply.

How does Michael feel about being known by his face, and not by his name? He said:

Well of course it's better to be remembered by your name, because it means your career has progressed a lot further. If you're remembered by your face and the parts you've played... that's one step. The other is a much bigger step. But to be honest I've not worried about this. I've not had sleepless nights. I've worked and that's all that really matters. You just do what you can, and take what you can. If stardom beckons, great, but if it doesn't, it's no use sitting around worrying.

It's incredible that an actor like Michael, so versatile and immensely talented, has never gotten the recognition he so richly deserves, and has never won an award or been given a prize of any kind. In a way, Michael lives in the shadow of fellow actor Peter Cushing, who also didn't receive the recognition he so richly deserved. If he had, Peter would most certainly have been knighted and become a Sir.

Michael Ripper relaxing at his home in Islington, North London, 1998.

Have they been ignored because of their connection with horror films? I will leave this up to you to decide.

Would Michael have ever liked to have received an award? "No," was his instant response.

> That part of life is a load of old nonsense to me. But I only have myself to blame really, as I never carried on

Michael Ripper in Hammer's *The Ugly Ducking* **(Columbia, 1959) a version of** *Dr. Jekyll and Mr. Hyde* **that has much in common with** *The Nutty Professor.*

for things like that. Being an actor was the only thing of any importance to me.

Michael has been in the business over 70 years and, sadly, seems to have been forgotten by the industry he served. No wonder he doesn't consider himself special.

Christopher Lee, like Robert Montgomery before him, tried to persuade Michael to go to Hollywood, as he said he would be in great demand and make a fortune. However, Michael was still not interested. He said:

> No, it definitely wasn't and isn't for me. I didn't want to go there in the 1950s, and I most certainly wouldn't want to go now. You see, I wouldn't want to die in Hollywood. I don't really want to die here, but I definitely wouldn't want to die over there.

Michael not only has a large following of admirers in this country, but in America as well, including some top Hollywood film directors such as Martin Scorsese, Joe Dante, John Carpenter and Steven Spielberg. While filming *Gremlins II* in Hollywood, Christopher Lee asked Steven Spielberg how he thought he should play his character in the movie. "Like Michael Ripper," Spielberg joked.

While Michael and his close family see him as just a regular guy, other people see Michael as a very talented, brilliantly clever character actor.

But what is a brilliantly clever character actor? Look at the way that Michael totally changed his face and whole appearance for many of his characters. He often played characters well beyond his own age. To be able to pull it off convincingly is extremely difficult. A great example is Eric the liftman in the classic St. Trinian's films. Michael looked completely different in person as opposed to how he appeared onscreen. He managed to take on the voice, face and physical appearance of an older and completely different person. I know this is the job of a character actor, but Michael pulled it off so convincingly that it was difficult to realize it was really Michael Ripper. He often used this ability for his many diverse portrayals.

No biography about Michael Ripper would be complete without mentioning a wonderful lady who plays a very important part in Michael's life these days. She is Michael's third wife, Cecelia Doidge-Ripper. Cecelia is wonderful for Michael—a tower of strength who keeps him physically active. She is perfect for him in every way and they are a happily united couple. It is thanks to Cecelia that Michael remains as active as he does. They visit her mother, someone whom he always enjoys meeting very much, and his beloved daughter Susan in Hampshire—where he even sits and chats with his first wife Jean. She also makes sure he keeps in contact with his brother Peter. Cecelia makes Michael smile, she brightens his life and jokes with him constantly. In return, Michael loves her dearly.

The first time Cecelia met Michael was on the set of the Yorkshire Television comedy series *Sir Yellow* in 1973. Over 20 years later on October 25, 1995, they married at Walton-on-Thames in London. Michael's old friend Norman Mitchell was one of the guests, and said, "I was honored to attend."

Before their marriage, Cecelia had lived with Michael and had been his partner for many years. When they first met she worked as a television costume designer, but today she does a completely different type of job which takes her only a short distance away from their home.

While living with Cecelia, Michael gave up smoking and drinking. He said:

> I used to make my own beer and my own wine, and drink a hell of a lot until quite recently. I never got drunk, but I used to drink a lot. Beer and wine were my favorites and sometimes I would drink whiskey, but it wasn't a regular attack. Anyway, I don't drink at all now, except other things besides alcohol. Another thing I did was smoke very heavily. I used to buy a round tin of 50 cigarettes every morning, and by evening I'd smoked the whole lot. But now I don't drink and I don't smoke. I don't feel any healthier for having given up. But certainly I wouldn't still be alive today if I still smoked and drank and did the things that I did in the old days.

Michael has made many friends within the business—many of whom have contributed to this biography. Over 10 years ago on Michael's 75th birthday, a surprise party was held. Not just to celebrate his birthday, but also his 60 years in show business. It was the idea of a long-standing friend and neighbor of the Rippers, the actress Peggy Mount O.B.E. [Order of the British Empire], who meets up with Michael and Cecelia regularly for a chat. Peggy first met Michael in 1957, when they appeared briefly together in the film *The Naked Truth*. For the surprise party Peggy was able to get together many of Michael's old friends, including Norman Mitchell, James Ellis, Bruce Montague, and many, many others too numerous to mention. Sadly, Christopher Lee was unable to attend, due to filming commitments.

But what a wonderful, kind, thoughtful thing for Peggy Mount to do. She, like many others, realizes what a very special person Michael is, and that he does deserve the respect and recognition of his peers. Michael himself was totally taken aback by the event. He said:

> I've worked with many stars in my time, I never thought I would be the star myself.

Recently at a Hammer Films gala event at the Barbican Cinemas in London, which was attended by many Hammer stars and fans, Christopher Lee delivered a speech which mentioned that Michael was sitting among the large audience. Lee made Ripper get to his feet, at which the audience gave the unassuming Michael a standing ovation, one that was richly deserved. No doubt Michael found the audience reaction to him somewhat hard to understand.

He was told that when people went to see Hammer Films in the 1950s and 1960s they would get up out of their seats and say, "Where is Michael Ripper?" They would shout for him if he didn't turn

Michael Ripper with his biographer, Derek Pykett at Bray on June 27, 1998

up in one of the films. When asked if he knew anything about this he replied, "No. I might have been there if I had."

There has been lots of talk recently about Hammer going back into production. If this did happen, and Michael was offered a role, would he accept it? "Yes" he said, "As long as they knew what they were up to." Did Michael think it was a good idea for the company to start up again? "No. They should leave it as it was," he replied.

Quite recently Michael turned up in a documentary on the Science Fiction Channel to celebrate 40 years of Hammer. He also made a surprise guest appearance in a documentary called *In Search of Dracula*. His appearance was definitely put there to surprise Hammer fans as he opened the church door at the beginning to let viewers inside. Jonathan Ross presented the above documentary from a Gothic church setting in

Anthony Hinds and Michael Ripper at the Bray reunion in 1998.

candlelight. During one of his speeches, Michael is in view polishing a chair. Jonathan suddenly mentions Hammer films and a big smile comes across Michael's face, and there is a twinkle in his eye. After which he happily polishes a candlestick.

During his over 70 years in show business, Michael has worked with most of the top stars of classic British cinema, and made many, many friends within the acting profession. He said:

> I have been very lucky really, to have been able to work with some wonderful people. Many of whom I became quite friendly with. If ever I worked with actors that were not so friendly, and not very approachable, I deliberately avoided them if possible. I must admit I've met some pretty dreadful people over the years I have been an actor. It's not nice to mention names. I wouldn't be able to remember half the names anyway.

Sadly today, due to memory problems, Michael is unable to recall many of the things that have happened during his life and career. Michael even finds it hard to remember his days at Hammer. He said:

> I've been in so many Hammer Films that I find it difficult today to sort one out from the other.

What Michael has been able to remember about Hammer and the rest of his career, as well as his private life, has been put into this biography. With the help of his wife, brother and daughter, it has been possible to piece together memories Michael was not so sure about.

Because of the difficulty of memorizing lines, Michael may never act again. He said:

> I would be letting myself down and other people. It just is not fair to mess people around. I think once you start being unable to remember lines, it's time to call it a day.

Michael also said:

> I have stopped being the actor I became. I cannot do anything about it now, and wouldn't really want to either. My whole acting character has gone, it lived in some other time.

Hopefully, Michael is wrong, and perhaps one day very soon some-one will persuade him back into the studios to give us one last classic, unforgettable Ripper performance.

Let 'er Rip
by John Stell

If you blink your eyes for a moment, you might miss him. After he's poured the drinks, dug the graves, interrogated the suspects, or delivered his fares to their destinations, his part may be over. Then again, perhaps he may prove most valuable to the protagonists: providing first aid, arranging publicity and travel plans, or aiding in the investigation, so that his presence extends beyond a mere five minutes. Whatever the size of the role, however, he gets your attention. Is it the twinkle in his eyes? Perhaps it's the cheeriness in his voice. He certainly has *something*.

Michael Ripper (left) in *These Dangerous Years* (1957) with Marty Wilde.

Brides of Dracula

Curse of the Werewolf

Night Creatures

The Phantom of the Opera

How else does one begin to understand the popularity of someone who played mostly supporting roles throughout his 60-plus-year film career? The answer: No matter what the part, Michael Ripper managed to convey that one aspect of what one suspects is a key trait of his real personality: charm.

Michael Ripper, affectionately known as The Rip, usually played characters listed by their occupation in the credits, e.g., "Stage Manager" in *Lady Godiva Rides Again* (1951), "Waiter" in both *The Green Man* (1956) and *The Punch and Judy Man* (1963), or "First Card Player" in *Moon Zero Two* (1969). Best known to most of us for his work in the Hammer horrors, one could find The Rip playing a sinister coachman in *Brides of Dracula* (1960), a comical cabby in *Phantom of the Opera* (1962) or a gruff landlord in *Scars of Dracula* (1970). His face became so familiar to us that we would swear this guy was in every Hammer

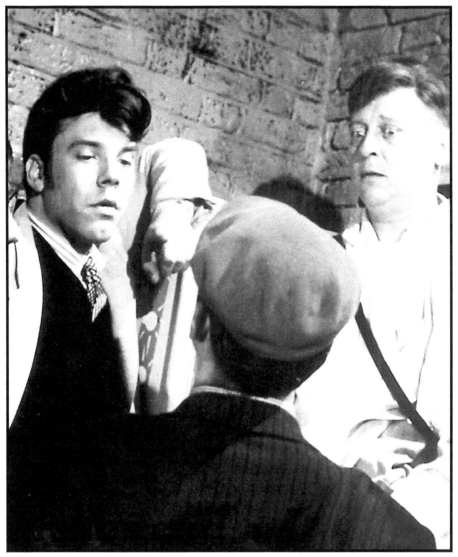

Michael Ripper played nine parts in *What a Crazy World* (1963) which starred Joe Brown. Ripper's character was "The Common Man" in this rock and roll movie.

horror film, even though this obviously wasn't the case. He certainly is considered part of the Hammer family, perhaps the kindly uncle who doesn't always make it to the reunions, by any fan of The Studio that Dripped Blood.

The Rip seemed to have a knack, at least in his horror efforts, for tending bar. As Max in *Dracula Has Risen from the Grave* (Hammer, 1968), for example, The Rip is his usual grinning self, standing on the

Michael Ripper (left) as the gruff landlord in *Scars of Dracula* (Hammer, 1970).

sidelines unaware of the evil that is going on around him. Amiable as always, he does what he can to help his employees, but his services are not required for aiding in the destruction of Dracula. Sometimes, however, these barkeeps were asked to do more than just provide refreshment for potential victims of vampires and the like. As Ernie the bartender in *Quatermass II* (Hammer, 1957), The Rip is called to do battle with aliens who have enslaved most of the town's population. While Ernie is a stern, serious bloke, he is noticeably the only one of the townspeople who doesn't whine and complain, but instead stands readily by, armed and prepared to do battle. He even helps blow up the main alien dome. While not the grinning, amiable chap he typically plays in other films, we still find ourselves watching him because of what he *doesn't* say. It is the quiet found in his performance (while others run around screaming and yelling) that draws our attention to him. With intense eyes and stoic expression, The Rip shows us his character is one of determination and conviction. In *The Deadly Bees* (Amicus, 1966), The Rip as David Hawkins not only slings alcohol, but also acts as Special Constable in a town plagued by bizarre bee attacks. Again, The Rip is very solemn and business-like, getting a chance at film's end to play the hero by aiding in the rescue of Suzanna Leigh.

Michael Ripper (right) as Tom Bailey, owner of the local pub in *The Reptile* (Hammer, 1966) pictured with Ray Barrett.

With respect to pubs, however, The Rip's best role can be found in *The Reptile* (Hammer, 1966). Here, The Rip is Tom Bailey, owner of the only pub in a small Cornish village plagued by mysterious deaths. When "strangers" come to town (relatives of one of the victims), Tom is the only one who shows them hospitality, even though they cleared out his bar. Even when his inn is cleared out a second time, Tom is still gracious. "Well, you've emptied my pub again, haven't you? I think you better buy a drink for yourself before you bankrupt me," he says grinning, not a hint of anger in his voice. It's a great line, delivered with sensitivity because Tom understands what is going on.

In fact, The Rip's role in *The Reptile* is certainly his most sensitive performance. "Just be careful, very careful," he warns, as if that's his final word on the matter. But later, he comes to the aid of Harry and

Valerie Spalding by not only helping to solve the mystery, but also rescuing Valerie from a burning mansion. More importantly, however, the Tom Bailey role is the most interesting of all the protagonists because he's the one who changes in the film. He tells Harry, "For the first time in my life I'm frightened." Yet he puts his fears aside and does the right thing. Harry, on the other hand, is introduced as a "stubborn" character and remains that way. He, unlike Tom, does not realize what he is up against. Thus, The Rip has taken what could have been the thankless, "second fiddle" role and punched it up with warmth, gentleness, and sensitivity, thereby becoming the true hero of the piece. It's a role that could have easily been overplayed, or gone by hardly noticed. But The Rip plays the role perfectly, with just the right amount humor and dread that makes barkeep Tom Bailey a memorable character.

Of course, The Rip could make memorable characters out of those who enjoyed spending time on the other side of the bar too. In 1958's *The Revenge of Frankenstein*, Hammer Film's sequel to *The Curse of Frankenstein* (1957), The Rip has a beautiful opening bit as a drunken graverobber named Kurt. Looking unkempt with long, greasy black hair, poor Kurt looks like he's about to pass out or throw up at any moment. At first hesitant to help his friend pinch Frankenstein's corpse ("There's nothing wrong with it. I just don't like it."), he's finally persuaded by the promise of a good night's pay. His matter-of-fact response of "You would," to his pal's asking if he would suggest any plan that might go wrong, always gets a laugh. Yes, The Rip plays a humorous and convincing drunk, but a most likable one.

In *The Mummy* (Hammer, 1959), The Rip is a poacher who, while setting traps, catches an eyes-wide glimpse of the bandaged beast. He rushes to the Red Lion to quench his fear ("Make it a large one.") and tells the patrons of his ordeal. "I've seen the likes tonight that mortal eyes shouldn't look at," he begins. "Ten foot tall, he was, swayed up in bandages, come lumbering through that wood like a great bear...I tell you it wasn't human." The Rip delivers these lines in a state of panic, anxiously turning his head from side to side, capping off the scene with, "I'll have another one of those." Later he's called to the police station to describe his ordeal, but thinks he's been caught poaching ("It was only a little hare"). The Rip brings generates more laughs via his indecision on how tall the mummy actually was ("Ten foot...maybe seven foot six..."). It's a bit daunting when the mummy's Egyptian helpmate viciously attacks this amiable poacher.

Michael Ripper (right) as a drunken graverobber named Kurt in *The Revenge of Frankenstein* **(Hammer, 1957).**

The Rip fares no better as the old soak in Hammer's *The Curse of the Werewolf* (1961). "It was no ordinary wolf, gentlemen," he tells a bar's patrons. "No ordinary wolf would tear out the throat and drink the blood." Again speaking of "strange things that should not be spoken of," The Rip finds himself in jail with Leon (Oliver Reed), the werewolf. The poor sot has no chance of escape. And in *The Curse of the Mummy's Tomb* (Hammer, 1964), The Rip, as an Egyptian helper named Achmed, belches and points to a sarcophagus, as if the mummy did it. Shortly thereafter, Achmed's body is found mangled in a crate.

What The Rip manages to do with his smaller roles is rather amazing if you think about it. Essentially he's playing the same part in these films: drunk sees monster, drunk spouts an eyewitness account, drunk dies. Sure, the make-up is different. The old soak has a head of white

Michael Ripper as the Japanese driver in *The Secret of Blood Island* (Hammer, 1965).

hair while the poacher wears a cap and is dirty-faced. Achmed is clad in traditional Egyptian garb. Still, The Rip makes each of these characters distinctive: the old soak speaks slowly and confidently, while the Poacher rattles along in a state of panic. Achmed hardly utters a word. Even looking at his bartender roles one can see how each is unique. David Hawkins is stern and officious; Max is amiable and friendly; and Tom Bailey is sensitive and concerned. The Rip finds a different approach to each role, despite the similarities, but still exudes that charm of his – that way he has of letting the viewer know he's enjoying himself.

Perhaps The Rip's turn as Longbarrow in *The Mummy's Shroud* (Hammer, 1967) is the best evidence of The Rip's impact on an audience. Longbarrow is, as you may recall, the quintessential brown-noser, fumbling and bumbling to please the rich, arrogant, and intolerable Stanley Preston ("Yes, sir…yes, Mr. Preston, yes sir…Thank you, sir…"). Preston frequently cuts him off in mid-sentence, shows him no respect, and basically treats Longbarrow as an annoying puppy dog. Still, we get the sense that Longbarrow knows the truth about Preston. In a perfectly timed comic moment, as Preston is dictating his discovery of the tomb and says, "Twice I had to hold [the mutinous workers] at gunpoint," The Rip stops writing, widens his eyes a bit, and glances over at Preston with a "you're full of it" look. Being the dutiful press liaison, he says nothing. As the danger mounts, and Preston plans to flee back to England, Longbarrow sheepishly asks, "Are you going to take me with you, sir?" When Preston says yes, Longbarrow gets positively giddy ("I'm so excited, I can't stop trembling."). But Preston must change his plans, and that includes not taking Longbarrow with him, reducing the easily intimidated fellow to tears.

Now one would think that a wimpy, spineless character like Longbarrow would not engage our sympathies. But this is where The Rip's strengths come into play. Somehow we get the sense that Longbarrow just wants to please his boss and be liked. He doesn't harm anyone; he's a pussycat. Perhaps he's dealt with Preston types his entire career. Ultimately, though, we learn Longbarrow is desperately homesick, which probably explains his "don't rock the boat" philosophy. We really feel for this guy when Preston kisses him off.

And this makes The Rip's death scene all the more tragic and shocking. It's certainly the most violent death scenario ever devised by Hammer for him. Waking from his sleep, Longbarrow clumsily breaks his glasses and bursts into tears. Opening the door, he doesn't realize that standing

in front him is the deadly mummy, who wraps Longbarrow up in his own bed sheets and hurls him to the streets below, as Longbarrow cries out for someone to help him. Longbarrow hits the edge of a trough, and we see the blood spray from his body. This is a particularly cruel fate for a character who hurt no one, and it is heartbreaking for the audience. Our Rip didn't deserve this! Again, as in *The Reptile*, The Rip steals the show from his fellow performers, making a secondary, basically comic character the one to watch.

Certainly The Rip's career, however, did not consist entirely of easygoing roles. He was the serious-minded inspector in *The Plague of the Zombies* (Hammer, 1966), trying to discover why bodies are disappearing from the graveyard. In *X—The Unknown* (Hammer, 1956), he plays the stern Sergeant Harry Grimsdyke. Because he is a military man caught in a crisis, there is little time for relaxing as radioactive mud threatens to destroy the countryside. Grimsdyke spends most of his time giving orders and organizing his men. Still, there are a couple of trademark Ripper grins to be found here. During a Geiger counter test, the last private to be tested is a bit of an underachiever. The Captain tells Grimsdyke, "Bury [the radioactive material] somewhere he won't take all day to find

Enemy from Space

The Curse of the Mummy's Tomb

The Mummy

The Plague of the Zombies

it." Grimsdyke responds, "Very good, sir," with a sly, knowing grin. He gives the Captain another grin after burying the material ("Shouldn't take long, sir."). Because these moments take place early in the film, we find ourselves looking out for Grimsdyke during the rest of the movie. Although The Rip is mostly in the background, he manages to get our attention, all because of a few well-placed smiles.

In their book *Hammer Films: An Exhaustive Filmography*, authors Tom Johnson and Deborah Del Vecchio claim The Rip's best role for Hammer can be found in *Captain Clegg*, aka *Night Creatures* (1962). As Mipps the coffin maker (and French brandy smuggler), The Rip makes his first appearance leading a choir. ("The choir sings in tune. Sometimes," Dr. Blyss [Peter Cushing] says.) When the English troops arrive to investigate the village, The Rip, a partner in crime, has plenty of opportunities to flash his patented "knowing grin," such as when the military search the bar, or the Captain interrogates Dr. Blyss, who is really the notorious pirate Captain Clegg. Best of all is The Rip's quip to the soldiers as they march off to follow up a lead: "Yes, these chilly nights are good for business. And if you get lost on the marshes it will be even better."

Captain Clegg is one of those films where the "villains" are actually the people we cheer for. Clegg uses the profits from the smuggling to

Many claim Michael Ripper's best role can be found in *Captain Clegg* **(Hammer, 1962).**

improve life in the village where he also provides spiritual comfort. And Mipps is his right-hand man. Mipps always looks like the proverbial cat that swallowed the canary, trying to remain polite and cordial to the investigators, while also feeling quite amused by the deception. The Rip's expressive eyes, wrinkled forehead, and slightly lowered head convey a man who has a secret he's trying to keep. When Clegg is killed during the climax, a tearful and loyal Mipps carries the body to the already-dug grave.

Looking at the strength of The Rip's work with respect to his fully realized roles, one may wonder why he wasn't given more opportunities to shine. But looking at his list of credits it's quite clear that during horror's renaissance in the 1960s, The Rip was a very busy man, doing anywhere from two to six films in a year, not including his television work. Sadly, as Hammer moved away from its Gothic-set horrors, The Rip was given less and less to do. Perhaps The Rip could have given a

The Chequers Manoeuver was a television play by Charlotte and Denis Plimmer, which was broadcast September 30, 1968 on the BBC. The secret group meets to plan an assassination. Ernest Clark, Ripper (kneeling), Derek Newark, Geoffrey Palmer and Anne Ridler star. Ripper's character's name was Richard M. Nixon.

much-needed boost to several of the latter-day Hammers. As he proved time and time again, his earnest performances provided some of the best moments in the films in which he participated.

Character actors are a breed taken for granted by most, not just the filmmakers, but the fans too. Luckily Michael Ripper spent much of his film career in a genre whose fans appreciate nearly every aspect of the filmmaking process. Any fan of British horror during the 1960s certainly knows the name and face of The Rip. And what a pleasant face it is! Whether he was wearing a mask of fear of amusement, The Rip gave something extra in his performances, never walking through any part, no matter how small. He always seemed to be enjoying himself, and thus, in return, the audiences for his films found The Rip a most enjoyable presence, even in the smallest doses. And with the recent Hammer video boom we can start keeping an eye out for him again. This time, however, our glasses will be raised to toast The Rip.

Michael Ripper and Christopher Lee had a touching reunion at the Monster Rally Opening Ceremony.

RIP

Michael Ripper passed away on June 28, 2000, almost a year after this biography was published and Mr. Ripper traveled to Washington D.C. for Monster Rally (July, 1999), which was his first visit to the U.S.

Fans went wild when Christopher Lee singled out Michael Ripper and brought him forward to the microphone. Ripper, who was suffering from Alzheimer's, a disease many families are dealing with, smiled with delight. It was obvious he remembered his old friend, Lee. Camera flashes made the ballroom seem like a night at the Academy Awards, and to the fans in attendance, it was even better. Michael Ripper died a year later, but he and his family were able to enjoy seeing his biography in print.

Michael Ripper at Monster Rally

Thanks for the Memories

(Letters from Three Fans)

Michael Ripper and Hammer Film Productions fit together like hand and glove and the two had a long and fruitful relationship lasting for 24 years and covering 35 films.

Whether his role was large, as in *The Reptile* (portraying his customary innkeeper) or small as in *Brides of Dracula* (another Ripper standby, a coachman), Michael Ripper gave the studio and his audience all he had, never disappointing either.

My own personal favorites from Mr. Ripper's Hammer Films are as follows:

His role as Max from *Dracula Has Risen from the Grave,* behaving quite parental to Paul (Barry Andrews) and quietly stealing every scene that he is in… Perhaps this explains why Christopher Lee's Dracula and Mr. Ripper don't share any scenes together, after all you wouldn't want the King of Vampires upstaged by an innkeeper—would you?

Mr. Ripper's strong performance as Mr. Mipps in *Captain Clegg* has always impressed me with the self-righteousness and pathos that he brought to the role. Peter Cushing's Clegg couldn't have asked for a better right hand man and because of the strength of these two great actors, the ending where Mipps carries Clegg to his grave is positively heart wrenching!

Much has been written about Mr. Ripper's excellent performance as Longbarrow in *The Mummy's Shroud* and I am in total agreement with them all! Mr. Ripper carries the film and turns an average creature film into something a little better than it deserves to be. His is the best performance, both comic and tragic, and he has one hell of a great death scene!

Besides the afore mentioned Hammer Films, Mr. Ripper also did fine work outside of Bray Studios; the one in particular that I love is the Amicus feature *Torture Garden.* In this thriller Mr. Ripper acted toe to toe with Hollywood heavyweights Burgess Meredith and Jack Palance.

Besides out-performing them, Mr. Ripper also manages to murder dear old Burgess—or so it seemed.

Besides his film work, Mr. Ripper has also enjoyed an extensive television career, and I did have the pleasure of viewing his wonderful performance as the sympathetic Chauffeur in the delightful BBC series *Butterflies*. Broadcast several years back on my local P.B.S. station, it was amazing to see Michael Ripper on a weekly basis! This series took full advantage of his dramatic and comedic skills and is a must for all fans of Mr. Ripper's great talent!

I hope it's become apparent that I'm a huge fan of the unique and fun Mr. Ripper, I know I could go on and on listing favorite performances from this wonderful man—but I would rather sum it up in this way:

To me, a Michael Ripper appearance in any film—but more especially a Hammer Film—is much like attending a family reunion and waiting for your favorite uncle to arrive. I mean everything's all going good and well but you just can't wait for that particular Uncle to pop in and spice things up ever so much. Also, everybody loves him dearly.

Thanks so much for the grand memories Uncle Michael.

Your Fan Forever,
Danny R. Fulce
Texas, U.S.A

Growing up addicted to horror films, it was easy to appreciate the likes of Peter Cushing and Christopher Lee and other leading actors, but I was still quite young when I started to notice another name that popped up in most of those great Hammer movies—Michael Ripper.

After I matched the name to the face, I realized that he was in all my favorite films. No coincidence there!

Even in the most fleeting roles, seeing Michael Ripper in a film is like seeing a dear old friend. It cheers you up, or makes you sad, or chills you. Whatever the role—I always believe him.

At a recent Hammer/Fanex convention at the Hunt Valley Inn, Baltimore, Maryland here in the U.S.A., *The Revenge of Frankenstein* was showing. Peter Cushing's name in the credits got a nice round of applause, second only to Michael Ripper who got a very nice hand and hoots and howlers of "Yeah, Michael" and "The Ripster" and stuff like that!

Now that my daughter has become a fan of classic British films, she too has learned the joy of playing "Where's Michael Ripper?" and recognizing his unmistakable face, voice and brilliant talent.

We'd both like to thank Michael Ripper for all of the joy and thrills and chills that he's given us, and continues to give us. Thank You!

Michael and Karmellah Howlett
Massachusetts, U.S.A.

"I've seen the like tonight that mortal eyes shouldn't look at…"

These now immortal words echoed around the darkness of the packed cinema, bringing a moment of light relief to those of us transfixed to the screen, as yet another Hammer horror unfolded before our eyes. It was March 1965 and myself and scores of others had once again enthusiastically paid our money to watch a re-run of *The Mummy* and see these masters at work on both sides of the camera.

Never onscreen, but true geniuses of their craft, Terence Fisher directed with intuitive and decisive flair, Jack Asher provided beautiful crisp photography, Bernard Robinson designed marvelous sets, Roy Ashton created stunning and realistic make-up, etc.

And immortalized on the screen before us, Peter Cushing, as the dashing hero John Banning, relentlessly pursuing the clues to his father's insanity and death, Christopher Lee imbuing the title creature with such menace and pathos without uttering a single word — and of course, "Good Old Michael Ripper!"

Because that's how Michael was known amongst us fans. Hammer's tales of horror were always so finely crafted that you could be sure that in amongst the thrills, action and suspense there would be one or two moments of welcome light relief, and such scenes were an integral part of their success. Many great actors graced such classic scenes, the likes of Sydney Bromley, Miles Malleson, Thorley Walters and others, but it's true to say that none so well, or as instantly recognizable, as Michael Ripper. He was and still is a master of his craft, giving performances which transcended the mere written word, and with a subtle raised eyebrow, a deft move of the hand, or quizzical look at the camera or a curl of a lip, brought a depth and sheer presence to the character that you felt added a truly vital element to the film's overall appeal. Indeed, very often it was an amusing scene such as that above, but we loved him for it, and the instant rapport and affection that we felt for the character matured over the years into admiration and respect for an actor who really is — in every sense — a one off [one-of-a-kind]. I can distinctly recall the cheers and hoots of delight that would thunder around the theatre at his appearance onscreen!

It was 1947 when Michael first made his appearance in a Hammer film, although in those days the company was still operating under the Exclusive banner. The film in question was *The Dark Road* and Michael was cast in his role by none other than James Carreras himself. It was the start of an association which would span 24 years, during which Michael appeared in 35 films for the company, seeing them reach both the heights of popularity and success, as well as the subsequent years of decline.

Released the same year as *The Curse of Frankenstein,* which secured Hammer's future for at least a decade, and written likewise by Jimmy Sangster, Michael appeared in arguably his first horror film for the company in an entertaining tale called *X—The Unknown.* Although not much more than a cameo appearance, this was followed a few months later in May 1956 by the filming of *Quatermass II* (U.S. title *Enemy from Space),* which was finally released almost a year later on May 24, 1957.

Quatermass II gives Michael an opportunity to shine the pub landlord (an occupation he would undertake frequently in roles to come), who assists the workers with an attack on the local base, eventually becoming trapped in the local complex. And it is Michael too who fires the grenade at the dome containing the creatures which eventually leads to the aliens' destruction—all in all, quite a part.

The following year Michael appeared in *The Revenge of Frankenstein.* Although only a small appearance at the start of the film as one of the graverobbers, the scene itself and Michael's performance in particular set the standard for years to come. As the old soak cajoled into digging up Frankenstein's body for 10 marks by his partner in crime Lionel Jeffries—who sits having his supper whilst Michael does all the digging and suchlike—the scene is a classic. Eventually uncovering the coffin (having already commented on the fact that he has never seen a Baron—and will they get any more for him in that case?!), this is heaved up onto the damp earth and a pair of crowbars used to pry open the lid, which falls backward. In peers Michael to get his first look at a Baron… "It's a priest—with no head!" This line is delivered with such skill, coupled with the facial expressions of shock along with the wide, bulging eyes, that it is always a joy to see. Marvelous entertainment, as Michael beats a hasty retreat from the scene!

We have already mentioned earlier Michael's role of the poacher in *The Mummy,* and following on from this he was given yet another cameo role as the coach driver in the 1960 film, *Brides of Dracula.* Here again his short performance of no more than five or six minutes is skillfully used to tremendous effect, as the coach driver bringing Yvonne Monlaur, as Marianne, to her fateful meeting with the vampire Baron Meinster. With top coat, hat and muffled scarf, croaking delivery of his lines, wide staring eyes and actions controlled and developed to a fine art, Michael presents us with a scene which is a forever favorite amongst fans. Hurriedly thundering along the dirt track through the forest, he brings the coach to an abrupt halt as he suddenly spots an obstacle lying across their path in the gloomy distance. Reluctantly stepping down he tries to gently calm the horses. "There's nothing to be scared of, nothing to be afraid of," he croaks (crossing himself in contradiction to his words!) as he holds onto the reins to try to placate the two animals, whilst glancing about him and staring out onto the gloom. Gingerly he takes a few steps forward to take a closer look… "Mother of God... It's a corpse!" The fact that it isn't, and merely a fallen tree-trunk, is really neither here nor there! It is the delivery of the lines and the performance overall that makes it the classic that it is. The same lines by another would not have anywhere near the impact, or entertainment, and yet with Michael he was able to make the whole scene his own.

Some of the many roles which followed over the years merely illustrated the unique talents of a man who is adept at being able to create the whole persona of a character with the minimal amount of screen time. Obviously realizing as much, Hammer made good use of his talents during the next decade, and all the parts he played merely illustrated what an integral part of Hammer's successful formula he was.

One of Michael's own favorite roles for Hammer (so far!) was that of the long-suffering Longbarrow in the 1966 film *The Mummy's Shroud*, in which he played the resigned manservant with such pathos and dignity that his death leaves a real vacuum in the film which is never adequately filled.

I would continue at some length, but suffice to say that it is an honor to be able to write a few words about a man who undoubtedly made a major contribution to the international success of Hammer films. With roles of great diversity, Michael Ripper brought us humor, sadness, thrills and excitement—and all played with total conviction—that provided so much enjoyment to so many. Which is why today his roles are remembered with such affection, and rightly regarded as classics of their time.

Is it any wonder why there is still today such thunderous applause when he appears—be it onscreen or off! We are privileged to be able to still watch him at work.

Brian Holland
Cornwall, England

Theatre

1929	The Ringer	(Grand Theatre, London)
	Belladonna	(Grand Theatre, London)
1930	Misalliance	(Old Court Theatre, London)
1935	Sheppey	(Theatre Royal, Rochdale)
	Sweeney Todd	(Theatre Royal, Rochdale)
1936	Macbeth	(Little Theatre, Leeds)
	Rich Man—Poor Man	(Arts Theatre, London)
	Little 'Ol Boy	(Arts Theatre, London)
1939	Yahoo	(Gate Theatre, Dublin
	A Murder Has Been Arranged	(Gate Theatre, Dublin)
	The Strange Lover	(Gate Theatre, Dublin)
	Dr. Faustus	(Gate Theatre, Dublin)
	The Rivals	(Gate Theatre, Dublin)
	The Cherry Orchard	(Gate Theatre, Dublin)
1943	Knock-Out	(Gate Theatre, Dublin)
	Hamlet	(Gate Theatre, Dublin)
1944	Show Boat	(Gaiety Theatre, Dublin)
	The Strings Are False	(Olympia Theatre, Dublin)
	Babes in the Wood	(Theatre Royal, Dublin)
1947	Boys in Brown	(Duchess Theatre, London)
	Pride Shall Have a Fall	(Arts Theatre, London)
1948	The Anatomist	(Westminster Theatre, London)
1952	World Without End	(Fortune Theatre, London)
1980	Worzel Gummidge	(Repertory Theatre, Birmingham)

Television

1947   Boys in Brown

1949   The Anatomist

1950   Drawing Room Detective
           The Cross and the Arrow
           The Undefeated

1951   The Strange Case of Hans Krantzer

1956   The Lark
           The Scarlet Pimpernel
           Fireside Theatre
           Douglas Fairbanks Presents
           Assignment Foreign Legion
           The Adventures of Aggie

1957   Mark Saber

1958   The Invisible Man
           Quatermass and the Pit
           Ivanhoe
           The Adventures of Robin Hood
           O.S.S.
           The Changing Years

1959   Dick and the Duchess
           Charlesworth
           Mario

1960   Scotland Yard
           Danger Man
           The Four Just Men
           Saber of London

1961   Knight Errant
       Maigret
       Sir Francis Drake

1962   Z-Cars

1963   Swallows and Amazons

1964   Sullivan Brothers

1965   Gideons Way

1966   Adam Adamant Lives!

1968   Journey to the Unknown
       The Saint
       Honey Lane
       The Chequers Manoeuvre

1969   Crimebuster

1970   Doomwatch
       Randall and Hopkirk (Deceased)
       Bright's Boffins
       Freewheelers

1971   Armchair Theatre

1972   New Scotland Yard
       Two Old Dears

1973   Hunter's Walk
       Melodrama
       Black Arrow
       Sir Yellow

1974   Happy Ever After
       Village Hall
       The Adventures of Black Beauty

1975   Hoggs Back
         Crown Court
         The Sweeney
         Churchill's People

1976   Coronation Street
         Worktalk

1977   The Two Ronnies
         The Upchat Line
         George and Mildred
         Miss Jones and Son
         The Other One

1978   Butterflies
         Born and Bred
         Chimpmates

1979   Sykes
         Cribb
         Le Petomaine
         Dawson Watch

1980   Worzel Gummidge
         Tales of the Unexpected

1981   Lady Killers
         Solo

1982   Playhouse
         If You Only Knew

1983   The Baker Street Boys

1984   Minder
         Missing from Home

1985   The Pickwick Papers

1986   In Sickness and in Health
       Unnatural Causes

1987   Home to Roost
       One by One
       Gruey

1988   The Gentlemans' Club

1989   Close to Home

1990   Jeeves and Wooster

1991   Little and Large Show

1995   The Bill
       Watford Gap
       Eastenders

Filmography

Twice Branded (1935)
Credits: Director: Maclean Rogers; Producer: George Smith; Screenplay: Kathleen Butler; Production Company: George Smith Enterprises; Distributor: RKO Radio Pictures

Cast: Robert Rendel (Charles Hamilton), James Mason (Henry Hamilton), Michael Ripper

Prison Breaker (1936)
Credits: Director: Adrian Brunel; Producer: George Smith; Screenplay: Frank Witty; Production Company: George Smith Enterprises; Distributor: Columbia Pictures

Cast: James Mason (Bunny Barnes), Ian Fleming (Stephen Shand), George Merritt (Goldring), Wally Patch (Villars), Michael Ripper

A Touch of the Moon (1936)
Credits: Director: Maclean Rogers; Producer: George Smith; Screenplay: Kathleen Butler; Production Company: George Smith Enterprises; Distributor: RKO Radio Pictures

Cast: John Garrick (Martin Barnaby), Dorthy Boyd (Mona Dupare), Joyce Bland (Mrs. Fairclough), Max Adrian (Francis Leverton), Wally Patch (Police Constable), Michael Ripper

Not so Dusty (1936)
Credits: Director: Maclean Rogers; Producer: George Smith; Screenplay: Kathleen Butler, H.F. Maltby, Wally Patch, Frank Atkinson; Production Company: George Smith Enterprises; Distributor: RKO Radio Pictures

Cast: Wally Patch (Dusty Gray), Gus McNaughton (Nobby Clark), Raymond Lovell (Mr. Holding), Michael Ripper

To Catch a Thief (1936)
Credits: Director: Maclean Rogers; Producer: George Smith; Screenplay: Kathleen Butler, H.F. Maltby; Production Company: George Smith Enterprises; Distributor: RKO Radio Pictures

Cast: John Garrick (John), Max Adrian (Salesman), Michael Ripper, Norman Pierce

Nothing Like Publicity (1936)
Credits: Director: Maclean Rogers; Producer George Smith; Screenplay: Kathleen Butler, H.F. Maltby; Production Company: George Smith Enterprises; Distributor: RKO Radio Pictures

Cast: William Hartnell (Pat Spencer), Max Adrian (Bob Wharncliffe), Michael Ripper

Busman's Holiday (1936)
Credits: Director: Maclean Rogers; Producer: George Smith; Screenplay: Kathleen Butler, H.F. Maltby; Production Company: George Smith Enterprises; Distributor: RKO Radio Pictures

Cast: Wally Patch (Jeff Pinkerton), Gus McNaughton (Alf Green), Robert Hobbs (Harry Blake), Norman Pierce (Crook), Michael Ripper (Crook)

The Heirloom Mystery (1936)
Credits: Director: Maclean Rogers; Producer: George Smith; Screenplay: Kathleen Butler; Production Company: George Smith Enterprises; Distributor: RKO Radio Pictures

Cast: Edward Rigby (Charles Marriott), Gus McNaughton (Alfred Fisher), Michael Ripper

All That Glitters (1936)
Credits: Director: Maclean Rogers; Producer: George Smith; Screenplay: Denison Clift; Production Company: George Smith Enterprises; Distributor: RKO Radio Pictures

Cast: Jack Hobbs (Jack Tolley), Kay Walsh (Eva Payne-Coade), Dick Francis (Derek Montague), Michael Ripper

Pearls Bring Tears (1937)
Credits: Director: Manning Haynes; Producer: George Smith; Screenplay: Roy Lockwood; Production Company: George Smith Enterprises; Distributor: Columbia Pictures

Cast: John Stuart (Harry Willshire), Dorothy Boyd (Madge Hart), Googie Withers (Doreen), Michael Ripper

Farewell to Cinderella (1937)
Credits: Director: Maclean Rogers; Producer: George Smith; Screenplay: Maclean Rogers, Kathleen Butler, H.F. Maltby; Production Company: George Smith Enterprises; Distributor: RKO Radio Pictures

Cast: Anne Pichon (Margaret), John Robinson (Stephen Morley), Michael Ripper

The Strange Adventures of Mr. Smith (1937)
Credits: Director: Maclean Rogers; Producer: George Smith; Screenplay: H.F. Maltby, Kathleen Butler; Production Company: George Smith Enterprises; Distributor: RKO Radio Pictures

Cast: Gus McNaughton (Will Smith/Black Patch), Eve Gray (Mrs. Maidie Smith), Michael Ripper

Fifty Shilling Boxer (1937)
Credits: Director: Maclean Rogers; Producer: George Smith; Screenplay: Guy Fletcher; Production Company: George Smith Enterprises; Distributor: RKO Radio Pictures

Cast: Bruce Seton (Jack Foster), Moore Marriott (Tim Regan), Eve Gray (Miriam Steele), Michael Ripper

Father Steps Out (1937)
Credits: Director: Maclean Rogers; Producer: George Smith; Screenplay: Kathleen Butler; Production Company: George Smith Enterprises; Distributor: RKO Radio Pictures

Cast: George Carney (Joe Hardcastle), Dinal Sheridan (Helen Hardcastle), Bruce Seton (Johnnie Miller), Elizabeth Kent (Joan), Michael Ripper

Why Pick on Me? (1937)
Credits: Director: Maclean Rogers; Producer: George Smith; Screenplay: H.F. Maltby & Kathleen Butler; Production Company: George Smith Enterprises; Distributor: RKO Radio Pictures

Cast: Wylie Watson (Sam Tippett), Jack Hobbs (Stretton), Max Adrian (Jack Mills), Elizabeth Kent (Bubbles), Michael Ripper

Racing Romance (1937)
Credits: Director: Maclean Rogers; Producer: George Smith; Screenplay:

John Hunter; Production Company: George Smith Enterprises; Distributor: RKO Radio Pictures

Cast: Bruce Seton (Harry Stone), Elizabeth Kent (Muriel Hanway), Ian Fleming (Martin Royce), Robert Hobbs (James Archer), Michael Ripper

Easy Riches (1937)
Credits: Director: Maclean Rogers; Producer: George Smith; Screenplay: John Hunter; Production Company: George Smith Enterprises; Distributor: RKO Radio Pictures

Cast: George Carney (Sam Miller), Gus McNaughton (Joe Hicks), Michael Ripper

Merely Mr. Hawkins (1938)
Credits: Director: Maclean Rogers; Producer: George Smith; Screenplay: John Hunter; Production Company: George Smith Enterprises; Distributor: RKO Radio Pictures

Cast: Eliot Makeham (Alfred Hawkins), Dinah Sheridan (Betty Hawkins), Max Adrian (Mr. Fletcher), Michael Ripper

Paid in Error (1938)
Credits: Director: Maclean Rogers; Producer: George Smith; Screenplay: Basil Mason, H.F. Maltby; Production Company: George Smith Enterprises; Distributor: Columbia Pictures

Cast: George Carney (Will Baker), Googie Withers (Jean Mason), Michael Ripper

Darts are Trumps (1938)
Credits: Director: Maclean Rogers; Producer: George Smith; Screenplay: Kathleen Butler, H.F. Maltby; Production Company: George Smith Enterprises; Distributor: RKO Radio Pictures

Cast: Eliot Makeham (Joe Stone), Nancy O'Neil (Mary Drake), Ian Colin (Harry), Muriel George (Mrs. Drake), H.F. Maltby (Stephen Sims), Michael Ripper

Luck of the Navy (1938)
Credits: Director: Norman Lee; Productions: Walter C. Mycroft; Screenplay: Clifford Grey; Production Company: Associated British Picture; Distributor: Pathe

Cast: Geoffrey Toone (Clive Stanton), Clifford Evans (Peel), Henry Oscar (Perrin), Doris Hare (Mrs. Maybridge), Nigel Stock, Michael Ripper

Romance A'La Carte (1938)
Credits: Director: Maclean Rogers; Producer: George Smith; Screenplay: Vera Allinson; Production Company: George Smith Enterprises; Distributor: RKO Radio Pictures

Cast: Leslie Perrins (Louis), Dorothy Boyd (Anne), Michael Ripper

If I Were Boss (1938)
Credits: Director: Maclean Rogers; Producer: George Smith; Screenplay: Basil Mason; Production Company: George Smith Enterprises; Distributor: Columbia Pictures

Cast: Bruce Seton (Steve), Googie Withers (Pat), Ian Fleming (Mr. Baltimore), Michael Ripper

Coming of Age (1938)
Credits: Director: Manning Haynes; Producer: George Smith; Screenplay: Paul White, Rowan Kennedy; Production Company: George Smith Enterprises; Distributor: Columbia Pictures

Cast: Eliot Makeham (Henry Strudwick), Joyce Bland (Isobel Strudwick), Ruby Miller (Julia Knight), Jimmy Hanley (Arthur Strudwick), Michael Ripper

His Lordship Regrets (1938)
Credits: Director: Maclean Rogers; Producer: George Smith; Screenplay: Kathleen Butler, H.F. Maltby; Production Company: Canterbury; Distributor: RKO Radio Pictures

Cast: Claude Hulbert (Lord Cavender), Eve Gray (Enid), Michael Ripper

Weddings Are Wonderful (1938)
Credits: Director: Maclean Rogers; Producer: George Smith; Screenplay: Kathleen Butler, H.F. Maltby; Production Company: Canterbury; Distributor: RKO Radio Pictures

Cast: June Clyde (Cora Sutherland), Esmond Knight (Guy Rogers), Bruce Seton (John Smith), George Carney (Mr. Rogers), Michael Ripper

His Lordship Goes to Press (1938)
Credits: Director: Maclean Rogers; Producer: George Smith; Screenplay: Kathleen Butler, H.F. Maltby; Production Company: Canterbury; Distributor: RKO Radio Pictures

Cast: June Clyde (Valerie Lee), Hugh Williams (Lord Bill Wilmer), Michael Ripper

You're the Doctor (1938)
Credits: Director: Roy Lockwood; Producer: George Smith; Screenplay: Beaufoy Milton, H.F. Maltby; Production Company: New Georgian; Distributor: British Independent

Cast: Barry K. Barnes (John Meriden), Googie Withers (Helen Firmstone), Gus McNaughton (Kemp), Bruce Seton (Appleby), Eliot Makeham (Prout), Michael Ripper

Miracles do Happen (1938)
Credits: Director: Maclean Rogers; Producer: George Smith; Screenplay: Kathleen Butler, Con West, Jack Marks; Production Company: George Smith Enterprises; Distributor: New Realm

Cast: Jack Hobbs (Barry Strangeways), Bruce Seton (Rodney), George Carney (Greenlaw), Michael Ripper

Blind Folly (1939)
Credits: Director: Reginald Denham; Producer: George Smith; Screenplay: H.F. Maltby; Production Company: George Smith Enterprises; Distributor: RKO Radio Pictures

Cast: Clifford Mollison (George Bunyard), Gus McNaughton (Professor Zozo), Elliot Mason (Aunt Mona), Roland Culver (Ford), Michael Ripper

Captain Boycott (1947)
Credits: Director: Frank Launder; Producer: Frank Launder, Sidney Gilliat; Screenplay: Frank Launder, Wolfgang Wilhelm, Paul Vincent Carroll, Patrick Campbell; Production Company: Individual Pictures; Distributor: General Film

Cast: Stewart Granger (Hugh Davin), Cecil Parker (Captain Boycott), Robert Donat (Charles Stewart Parnell), Mervyn Johns (Watty Connell), Alastair Sim (Father McKeogh), Noel Purcell (Daniel McGinty), Niall MacGinnis (Mark Killian), Maurice Denham (Lt. Col; Strickland), Eddie Byrne (Sean Kerin), Ian Fleming (Times Correspondent), Michael Ripper (Pat Nolan)

The Dark Road (1947)
Credits: Director: Alfred Goulding; Producer: Henry Halstead; Screenplay: Henry Halstead; Production Company: Marylebone; Distributor: Exclusive Films

Cast: Charles Stuart (Sidney Robertson), Joyce Linden (Ann), Michael Ripper, Cyril Chamberlain, Sydney Bromley

Noose (1948)
Credits: Director: Edmond T. Greville; Producer: Edward Dryhurst; Screenplay: Richard Llewellyn, Edward Dryhurst; Production Company: Edward Dryhurst; Distributor: Pathe

Cast: Carole Landis (Linda Medbury), Derek Farr (Jumbo Hoyle), Stanley Holloway (Inspector Rendall), Nigel Patrick (Bar Gorman), Edward Rigby (Slush), John Salew (Greasy Anderson), Michael Ripper (Nelson), John Harvey

Oliver Twist (1948)
Credits: Director: David Lean; Producer: Anthony Havelock-Allan; Screenplay: David Lean, Stanley Haynes; Production Company: Cineguild; Distributor: General Film

Cast: Robert Newton (Bill Sykes), Alec Guinness (Fagin), Kay Walsh (Nancy), John Howard Davies (Oliver Twist), Anthony Newley (Artful Dodger), Hattie Jacques (Singer), Kathleen Harrison (Mrs. Sowerberry), Maurice Denham (Chief of Police), Diana Dors (Charlotte), Michael Ripper (Barney)

The Adventures of P.C. 49 (1949)
Credits: Director: Godfrey Grayson; Producer: Anthony Hinds; Screenplay: Alan Stranks, Vernon Harris; Production Company: Hammer Film Productions; Distributor: Exclusive Films

Cast: Hugh Latimer (Archibald Berkeley-Willoughby), Patricia Cutts (Joan), Michael Ripper (Fingers), Martin Benson (Skinny Ellis)

A Case for P.C. 49 (1949)
Credits: Director: Francis Searle; Producer: Anthony Hinds; Screenplay: Alan Stranks, Vernon Harris; Production Company: Hammer Film Productions; Distributor: Exclusive Films

Cast: Brian Reece (Archibald Berkeley-Willoughby), Michael Balfour (Chubby Price), Michael Ripper (George Steele)

Dr. Morelle—The Case of the Missing Heiress (1949)
Credits: Director: Godfrey Grayson; Producer: Anthony Hinds; Screenplay: Roy Plomley, Ambrose Grayson; Production Company: Hammer Film Productions; Distributor: Exclusive Films

Cast: Valentine Dyall (Dr. Morelle), Julia Lang (Miss Frayle), Philip Leaver (Samuel Kimber), Jean Lodge (Cynthia Mason), Peter Drury (Peter), Michael Ripper

The History of Mr. Polly (1949)
Credits: Director: Anthony Pelissier; Producer: John Mills; Screenplay: Anthony Pelissier; Production Company: Two Cities; Distributor: General Film

Cast: John Mills (Alfred Polly), Sally Ann Howes (Cristabel), Megs Jenkins (Plump Woman), Finlay Currie (Uncle Jim), Edward Chapman (Mr. Johnson), Shelagh Fraser (Minnie), Miles Malleson (Old Gentleman), Doris Hare (May Punt), Dandy Nichols (Mrs. Johnson), Irene Handl (Lady), Edie Martin (Lady on Roof), Cyril Smith (Mr. Voules), Juliet Mills (Little Polly), Michael Ripper (Shop Worker)

The Rocking Horse Winner (1949)
Credits: Director: Anthony Pelissier; Producer: John Mills; Screenplay: Anthony Pelissier; Production Company: Two Cities; Distributor: Rank

Cast: Valerie Hobson (Hester Grahame), John Howard Davies (Paul Grahame), John Mills (Bassett), Cyril Smith (The Bailiff), Michael Ripper (Chauffeur)

Your Witness (1950)
Credits: Director: Robert Montgomery; Producer: David E. Rose, Joan Harrison; Screenplay: Hugo Butler, Ian Hunter, William Douglas Home; Production Company: Coronado; Distributor: Warner Bros.

Cast: Robert Montgomery (Adam Heyward), Michael Ripper (Sam Baxter), Leslie Banks (Summerfield), Felix Aylmer (Judge), Andrew Cruickshank (Sir Adrian Horth), Jenny Laird (Mary Baxter), Shelagh Fraser (Ellen Foster), Stanley Baker (Bannoch), Richard Wattis

Old Mother Riley's Jungle Treasure (1951)
Credits: Director: Maclean Rogers; Producer: George Minter; Screenplay: Val Valentine; Production Company: Oakland Films; Distributor: Renown

Cast: Arthur Lucan (Mother Riley), Kitty McShane (Kitty), Sebastian Cabot (Morgan the Pirate), Cyril Chamberlain (Daincourt), Peter Butterworth (Steve), Michael Ripper (Jake)

Lady Godiva Rides Again (1951)
Credits: Director: Frank Launder; Producer: Frank Launder, Sidney Gilliat; Screenplay: Frank Launder, Val Valentine; Production Company: London Films; Distributor: British Lion

Cast: Dennis Price (Simon Abbott), John McCallum (Larry Burns), Stanley Holloway (Mr. Clark), Pauline Stroud (Marjorie Clark), George Cole (Johnny), Diana Dors (Dolores August), Eddie Byrne (Eddie Mooney), Kay Kendall (Sylvie), Dora Bryan (Publicity Woman), Alastair Sim (Hawtrey Murrington), Sidney James (Lew Beeson), Cyril Chamberlain (Harry), John Harvey (Buller), Richard Wattis (Casting Director), Michael Ripper (Stage Manager), Toke Townley, Googie Withers, Trevor Howard, Joan Collins

Secret People (1952)
Credits: Director: Thorold Dickinson; Producer: Sidney Cole; Screenplay: Thorold Dickinson, Wolfgang Wilhelm, Christianna Brand; Production Company: Ealing Studios; Distributor: General Film

Cast: Valentina Cortesa (Marie Brentano), Audrey Hepburn (Nora Brentano), Megs Jenkins (Penny), Bob Monkhouse (Barber), Michael Ripper, Sam Kydd

Derby Day (1952)
Credits: Director: Herbert Wilcox; Producer: Herbert Wilcox, Maurice Cowan; Screenplay: Monckton Hoffe, John Baines, Alan Melville; Production Company: Wilcox-Neagle; Distributor: British Lion

Cast: Anna Neagle (Lady Helen Forbes), Michael Wilding (David Scott), Googie Withers (Betty Molloy), John McCallum (Tommy Dillon), Peter Graves (Gerald Berkeley), Alfie Bass (Spider Wilkes), Nigel Stock (Jim Molloy), Richard Wattis (Editor), Sam Kydd, Michael Ripper

Treasure Hunt (1952)
Credits: Director: John Paddy Carstairs; Producer: Anatole de Grunwald; Screenplay: Anatole de Grunwald; Production Company: Romulus; Distributor: British Lion

Cast: Martita Hunt (Aunt Anna Rose), Jimmy Edwards (Hercules Ryall/Sir Roderick), Miles Malleson (Mr. Walsh), Toke Townley (William Burke), Irene Handl, Michael Ripper, Fred Johnson, Alfie Bass

Alf's Baby (1952)
Credits: Director: Maclean Rogers; Producer: John Harlow; Screenplay: A.P. Dearsley; Production Company: ACT Films; Distributor: Adelphi

Cast: Jerry Desmonde (Alf Donkin), Pauline Stroud (Pamela Weston), Peter Hammond (Tim Barton), Sebastian Cabot, Michael Ripper

Folly to Be Wise (1952)
Credits: Director: Frank Launder; Producer: Frank Launder, Sidney Gilliat; Screenplay: Frank Launder, John Dighton; Production Company: London Films; Distributor: British Lion

Cast: Alastair Sim (Captain Paris), Roland Culver (George Prout), Martita Hunt (Lady Dodds), Miles Malleson (Dr. Hector McAdam), Edward Chapman (Joseph Byres), Janet Brown (Jessie Killigrew) Robin Bailey (Intellectual), Michael Ripper (Corporal), Cyril Chamberlain (Drill Sergeant), George Cole (Private), Catherine Finn

Appointment in London (1952)
Credits: Director Philip Leacock; Producer: Maxwell Setton, Aubrey Baring; Screenplay: John Wooldridge, Robert Westerby; Production Company: May-flower; Distributor: British Lion

Cast: Dirk Bogarde (Tim Mason), Dinah Sheridan (Eve Canyon), Bryan Forbes (The Brat), Charles Victor (Dobbie), Richard Wattis (Pascal), Sam Kydd (Ackroyd), Michael Ripper (Bomb Aimer)

The Story of Gilbert and Sullivan (1953)
Credits: Director: Sidney Gilliat; Producer: Frank Launder, Sidney Gilliat; Screenplay: Sidney Gilliat, Leslie Baily; Production Company: London Films; Distributor: British Lion

Cast: Robert Morley (W.S. Gilbert), Maurice Evans (Arthur Sullivan), Eileen Herlie (Helen Lenoir), Peter Finch (Richard D'Oyley Carte), Dinah Sheridan (Grace Marston), Wilfrid Hyde-White (Mr. Marston), Michael Ripper (Louis), Richard Warner (Cellier), Leonard Sachs (Smythe), George Woodbridge (Reporter)

The Intruder (1953)
Credits: Director: Guy Hamilton; Producer: Ivan Foxwell; Screenplay: Robin Maugham, John Hunter, Anthony Squire; Production Company: Ivan Foxwell; Distributor: British Lion

Cast: Jack Hawkins (Wolf Merton), Michael Medwin (Ginger Edwards), George Cole (John Summers), Dennis Price (Leonard Perry), Duncan Lamont (Donald Cope), George Baker (Adjutant), Richard Wattis (School Master), Dora Bryan (Dora Bee), Patrick Barr (Inspector Williams), Edward Chapman (Walter Lowden), Michael Ripper

Blood Orange (1954)
Credits: Director: Terence Fisher; Producer: Michael Carreras; Screenplay: Jan Read; Production Company: Hammer Film Productions; Distributor: Exclusive Films

Cast: Ton Conway (Private Eye), Eric Pohlmann (Mercedes), Richard Wattis (Macleod), Delphi Lawrence (Chelsea), Michael Ripper, Roger Delgado

The Rainbow Jacket (1954)
Credits: Director: Basil Dearden; Producer: Michael Relph; Screenplay: T.E.B. Clarke; Production Company: Ealing Studios; Distributor: General Film

Cast: Robert Morley (Lord Logan), Kay Walsh (Barbara Crain), Bill Owen (Sam Lilley), Charles Victor (Mr. Ross), Honor Blackman (Monica Tyler), Wilfrid Hyde-White (Lord Stoneleigh), Sidney James (Harry), Sam Kydd (Bruce), Michael Ripper (Benny Loder), Katie Johnson, David Hemmings, Glyn Houston

The Belles of St. Trinian's (1954)
Credits: Director: Frank Launder; Producers: Frank Launder, Sidney Gilliat; Screenplay: Frank Launder, Sidney Gilliat; Production Company: London Films; Distributor: British Lion

Cast: Alastair Sim (Millicent, Clarence Fritton), Joyce Grenfell (Ruby Gates), George Cole (Flash Harry), Eric Pohlmann (Sultan of Makyad), Beryl Reid (Miss Dawn), Richard Wattis (Manton Bassett), Michael Ripper (Albert Faning), Irene Handl, Joan Sims, Sidney James, Michael Balfour, Barbara Windsor

A Tale of Three Women (1954)
Credits: Director Paul Dickson, Thelma Connell; Producers: Edward J. Danziger, Harry Lee Danziger; Screenplay: Paul Tabori, James Eastwood, George Mikes; Production Company: Danzigers; Distributor: Paramount Pictures

Cast: Derek Bond (Con-Man), Hazel Court (Lady Accomplice), Jack Watling (Kleptomaniac), Catherine Finn, Michael Ripper

The Sea Shall Not Have Them (1954)
Credits: Director: Lewis Gilbert; Producer: Daniel M. Angel; Screenplay: Lewis Gilbert, Vernon Harris; Production Company: Daniel M. Angel; Distributor: Eros

Cast: Michael Redgrave (Waltby), Dirk Bogarde (Mackay), Jack Watling (Harding), Anthony Steel (Treherne), Nigel Patrick (Slingsby), George Ross

(Tebbitt), Victor Maddern (Gus Westover), Michael Ripper (Botterill), Glyn Houston (Knox), Michael Balfour (Dray), Eddie Byrne (Porter), Anton Diffring (German Pilot), Nigel Green (Howard), Joan Sims (Hilda Tebbitt)

Geordie (1955)
Credits: Director: Frank Launder; Producers: Frank Launder, Sidney Gilliat; Screenplay: Sidney Gilliat, Frank Launder; Production Company: Argonaut; Distributor: British Lion

Cast: Alastair Sim (The Laird), Bill Travers (Geordie MacTaggart/Gamekeeper), Molly Urquhart (Geordie's Mother), Francis de Wolff (Henry Samson), Brian Reese (Dick Harley), Raymond Huntley (Rawlins), Miles Malleson (Lord Paunceton/ Olympic Squad Head), Stanley Baxter (Postman), Michael Ripper

Secret Venture (1955)
Credits: Director: R.G. Springsteen; Producer: William N. Boyle, Screenplay: Paul Erickson, Kenneth R. Hayles; Production Company: Republic; Distributor: Republic

Cast: Kent Taylor (Ted O'Hara), Kathleen Byron (Renee), Frederick Valk (Otto Weber), Maurice Kaufmann (Dan Fleming), Michael Balfour (Stevens), Michael Ripper

The Constant Husband (1955)
Credits: Director: Sidney Gilliat; Producers: Sidney Gilliat, Frank Launder; Screenplay: Sidney Gilliat, Val Valentine; Production Company: London Films; Distributor: British Lion

Cast: Rex Harrison (Charles Hathaway), Margaret Leighton (Miss Chesterman), Kay Kendall (Monica), Cecil Parker (Llewellyn), George Cole (Luigi Sopranelli), Raymond Huntley (Hassett), Michael Hordern (Judge), Eric Pohlmann (Papa Sopranelli), Charles Lloyd Pack (Solicitor), Ursula Howells (Miss Pargiter), Sam Kydd (Adelphi Barman), Michael Ripper (Left Luggage Attendant), George Woodbridge (Old Bailey Warder)

Richard III (1955)
Credits: Producer/Director: Laurence Olivier and Anthony Bushell; Screenplay: Alan Dent, Laurence Olivier, Colley Cibber and David Garrick; Based on the Play by William Shakespeare; Production Company: London Films; Distributor: Lopert

Cast: Laurence Olivier (Richard III), Ralph Richardson (Buckingham), Claire Bloom (Lady Anne), John Gielgud (Clarence), Cedric Hardwicke (Edward IV),

Alec Clunes (Hastings), Stanley Baker (Henry Tudor), Michael Gough (Dighton), Laurence Naismith (Stanley), Norman Wooland (Catesby), John Laurie (Lovel), Esmond Knight (Ratcliffe), Andrew Cruickshank (Brakenbury), Douglas Wilmer (Dorset), Michael Ripper (Second Murderer), George Woodbridge (Lord Mayor), Willoughby Gray (Priest), Patrick Troughton (Tyrell)

A Man on the Beach (1955)
Credits: Director: Joseph Losey; Producer: Anthony Hinds; Screenplay: Jimmy Sangster; Production Company: Hammer Film Productions; Distributor: Exclusive Films

Cast: Donald Wolfit (Carter), Michael Medwin (Max), Michael Ripper (Chauffeur)

X—The Unknown (1956)
Credits: Director: Leslie Norman; Producer: Anthony Hinds; Screenplay: Jimmy Sangster; Production Company: Hammer Film Productions; Distributor: Exclusive Films

Cast: Dean Jagger (Dr. Adam Royston), Edward Chapman (Elliot), Leo McKern (McGill), Anthony Newley (Private "Spider" Webb), William Lucas (Peter Elliot), Peter Hammond (Bannerman), Ian McNaughton ("Haggis"), Michael Ripper (Sergeant Harry Grimsdyke), John Harvey (Major Cartwright), Edwin Richfield (Old Soldier), Kenneth Cope (Private Lancing), Fraser Hines (Ian), Edward Judd (Soldier)

Reach for the Sky (1956)
Credits: Director: Lewis Gilbert; Producer: Daniel M. Angel; Screenplay: Lewis Gilbert, Vernon Harris; Production Company: Pinnacle; Distributor: Rank

Cast: Kenneth More (Douglas Bader), Alexander Knox (Mr. Joyce), Jack Watling (Peel), Nigel Green (Streatfield), Eddie Byrne (Sergeant Mills), Michael Ripper (Aeroplane Mechanic), Eric Pohlmann (Adjutant of Prison Camp), Michael Gough (Flying Instructor), Sam Kydd, Anton Diffring, Clive Revill, Michael Balfour

The Green Man (1956)
Credits: Directors: Robert Day, Basil Dearden; Producers: Frank Launder, Sidney Gilliat; Screenplay: Frank Launder, Sidney Gilliat; Production Company: Grenadier; Distributor: British Lion

Cast: Alastair Sim (Hawkins), George Cole (Blake), Terry-Thomas (Charles Broughtflower), Raymond Huntley (Sir George Upshoft), Dora Bryan (Lily), Cyril Chamberlain (Sergeant Bassett), Richard Wattis (Doctor), Arthur Brough (Landlord), Arthur Lowe (Radio Salesman), Michael Ripper (Waiter), Terence Alexander

Yield to the Night (1956)
Credits: Director: J. Lee Thompson; Producer: Kenneth Harper; Screenplay: John Cresswell, Joan Henry; Production Company: Associated British Picture; Distributor: Pathe

Cast: Diana Dors (Mary Hilton), Yvonne Mitchell (MacFarlane), Michael Craig (Jim Lancaster), Geoffrey Keen (Chaplain), Liam Redmond (Doctor), Molly Urquhart (Mason), Michael Ripper (Roy), Mona Washbourne (Mrs. Thomas), Marianne Stone (Richardson), Charles Lloyd Pack (Lawyer), Dandy Nichols (Mrs. Price), Shirley Ann Field

1984 (1956)
Credits: Director: Michael Anderson; Producer: N. Peter Rathvon; Screenplay: William P. Templeton, Ralph Gilbert Bettinson; Production Company: Holiday; Distributor: Pathe

Cast: Michael Redgrave (General O'Conner), Edmond O'Brien (Winston Smith), Mervyn Johns (Jones), Donald Pleasence (Parsons), Ernest Clark (Outer Party Announcer), Patrick Allen (Inner Party Official), Michael Ripper (Outer Party Orator), Kenneth Griffith (Prisoner), Ewen Solon

These Dangerous Years (1957)
Credits: Director: Herbert Wilcox; Producer: Anna Neagle; Screenplay: Jack Trevor Story; Production Company: Everest, Anna Neagle; Distributor: Pathe

Cast: George Baker (Padre), Frankie Vaughan (Dave Wyman), Thora Hird (Mrs. Larkin), Eddie Byrne (Danny), Kenneth Cope (Juggler), John Le Mesurier (Commanding Officer), David Lodge (Sergeant Lockwood), Michael Ripper (Private Simpson)

Not Wanted on Voyage (1957)
Credits: Director Maclean Rogers; Producers: Henry Halsted, Jack Marks; Screenplay: Michael Pertwee, Evadne Price, Roland Pertwee, Jack Marks; Production Company: Byron, Ronald Shiner; Distributor: Renown

Cast: Ronald Shiner (Steward Higgins), Brian Rix (Steward Hollebone), Eric Pohlmann (Pedro), Michael Ripper (Steward Macy)

Woman in a Dressing Gown (1957)
Credits: Director: J. Lee Thompson; Producers: J. Lee Thompson, Frank Godwin; Screenplay: Ted Willis; Production Company: Godwin-Willis; Distributor: Pathe

Cast: Yvonne Mitchell (Amy Preston), Anthony Quayle (Jim Preston), Sylvia Syms (Georgie Harlow), Andrew Ray (Brian Preston), Michael Ripper (Pawnbroker), Marianne Stone (Hairdresser), Melvyn Hayes (Newsboy)

The One that Got Away (1957)
Credits: Director: Roy Baker; Producer: Julian Wintle; Screenplay: Howard Clewes; Production Company: Rank; Distributor: Rank

Cast: Hardy Kruger (Franz Von Werra), Michael Goodliffe (RAF Interrogator), Terence Alexander (RAF Intelligence Officer), Alec McCowen (Duty Officer Hucknall), John Van Eyssen, Frederick Jaeger, Stratford Johns, Glyn Houston, Michael Ripper

Blue Murder at St. Trinian's (1957)
Credits: Director: Frank Launder; Producers: Frank Launder, Sidney Gilliat; Screenplay: Frank Launder, Sidney Gilliat, Val Valentine; Production Company: British Lion; Distributor: British Lion

Cast: Terry-Thomas (Captain Romney Carlton-Ricketts), George Cole (Flash Harry), Joyce Grenfell (Ruby Gates), Alastair Sim (Miss Fritton), Lionel Jeffries (Joe Mangan), Eric Barker (Culpepper Brown), Richard Wattis (Manton Bassett), Thorley Walters (Major), Michael Ripper (Liftman), Kenneth Griffith (Charlie Bull), Terry Scott (Sergeant), Ferdy Mayne, Cyril Chamberlain, Charles Lloyd Pack

The Naked Truth (1957)
Credits: Director: Mario Zampi; Producer: Mario Zampi; Screenplay: Michael Pertwee; Production Company: Anglofilm; Distributor: Rank

Cast: Terry-Thomas (Lord Mayley), Peter Sellers (Sonny MacGregor), Peggy Mount (Flora Ransom), Shirley Eaton (Belinda Right), Dennis Price (Michael Dennis), Joan Sims (Ethel Ransom), Miles Malleson (Reverend Bastable), Kenneth Griffith (Porter), Wally Patch (Fred), Wilfrid Lawson (Sergeant Rumbold), George Benson (Photographer), David Lodge (Policeman), Michael Ripper (Shopkeeper), Marianne Stone

Quatermass II (1957) (U.S. title: **Enemy from Space**)
Credits: Director: Val Guest; Producer: Anthony Hinds; Screenplay: Nigel Kneale, Val Guest; Production Company: Hammer Film Productions; Distributor: United Artists

Cast: Brian Donlevy (Quatermass), Sidney James (Jimmy Hall), Bryan Forbes (Marsh), William Franklyn (Brand), Vera Day (Sheila), Charles Lloyd Pack (Dawson), John Van Eyssen (The PRO), Percy Herbert (Gorman), Michael Ripper (Ernie), Marianne Stone (Secretary), Edwin Richfield (Peterson), George Merritt (Super), Michael Balfour (Harry)

The Steel Bayonet (1957)
Credits: Director: Michael Carreras; Producer: Michael Carreras; Screenplay: Howard Clewes; Production Company: Hammer Film Productions; Distributor: United Artists

Cast: Leo Genn (Major Gerrard), Michael Medwin (Vernon), Robert Brown (Sergeant Major Gill), Michael Ripper (Private Middleditch), Percy Herbert (Clark), Barry Lowe (Ferguson), Michael Balfour (Thomas)

I Only Arsked (1958)
Credits: Director: Montgomery Tully; Producer: Anthony Hinds; Screenplay: Sid Colin, Jack Davies; Production Company: Hammer Film Productions; Distributor: Columbia Pictures

Cast: Michael Medwin (Springer), Bernard Bresslaw (Popeye Poppiewell), Alfie Bass (Excused Boots Bisley), Charles Hawtrey (Professor), Norman Rossington (Cupcake Cook), David Lodge (Sergeant Potty Chambers), Michael Bentine (Fred), Francis Matthews (Mahmoud), Marne Maitland (King Fazim), Michael Ripper (Azim), Wolfe Morris (Salaman)

Girls at Sea (1958)
Credits: Director: Gilbert Gunn; Producers: Vaughan N. Dean, Gilbert Gunn; Screenplay: T.J. Morrison, Gilbert Gunn; Production Company: Associated British Picture; Distributor: Associated British Picture

Cast: Guy Rolfe (Captain), Ronald Shiner (Marine Ogg), Michael Hordern (Hewitt), Fabia Drake (Lady Hewitt), Lionel Jeffries (Tourist), Daniel Massey (Flag Lieutenant), David Lodge (Duckett), Warren Mitchell, Michael Ripper, Brian Wilde, Harold Goodwin, Richard Briers, Ian Holm

The Revenge of Frankenstein (1958)
Credits: Director: Terence Fisher; Producer: Anthony Hinds; Screenplay: Jimmy Sangster, Hurford Janes; Production Company: Hammer Film Productions; Distributor: Columbia Pictures

Cast: Pete Cushing (Doctor Victor Stein), Francis Matthew (Doctor Hans Kleve), Eunice Gayson (Margaret), Michael Gwynn (Karl), Lionel Jeffries (Fritz), Richard Wordsworth (Up Patient), Charles Lloyd Pack (President), George Woodbridge (Janitor), Michael Ripper (Kurt), Michael Mulcaster (Tattooed Man)

Camp on Blood Island (1958)
Credits: Director: Val Guest; Producer: Anthony Hinds; Screenplay: Jon Manchip White, Val Guest; Production Company: Hammer Film Productions; Distributor: Columbia Pictures

Cast: Carl Mohner (Piet Van Elst), Andre Morell (Colonel Lambert), Barbara Shelley (Kate Keiller), Michael Goodliffe (Father Anjou), Michael Gwynn (Tom Shields), Richard Wordsworth (Doctor Keiller), Edwin Richfield (Sergeant Major), Marne Maitland (Captain Sakamura), Wolfe Morris (Interpreter), Lee Montague (Japanese Officer Nangdon), Barry Lowe (Corporal Betts), Michael Ripper (Japanese Officer), Geoffrey Bayldon (Foster)

Up the Creek (1958)
Credits: Director: Val Guest; Producer: Henry Halsted; Screenplay: Val Guest, John Warren, Len Heath; Production Company: Byron, Hammer Film Productions; Distributor: Warner Bros.

Cast: David Tomlinson (Humphrey Fairweather), Peter Sellers (Bosun Docherty), Wilfrid Hyde-White (Foley), Vera Day (Lily), Michael Goodliffe (Nelson), Lionel Jeffries (Steady Barker), Sam Kydd (Bates), Patrick Cargill (Commander), Michael Ripper (Decorator), Barry Lowe (Webster), Edwin Richfield (Bennett), David Lodge (Scouse)

Further Up the Creek (1958)
Credits: Director: Val Guest; Producer: Henry Halsted; Screenplay: Val Guest, John Warren, Len Heath; Production Company: Byron, Hammer Film Productions; Distributor: Columbia Pictures

Cast: David Tomlinson (Humphrey Fairweather), Frankie Howerd (Bos'n), Shirley Easton (Jane), Thora Hird (Mrs. Galloway), Lionel Jeffries (Steady Barker), Sam Kydd (Bates), David Lodge (Scouse), Esma Cannon (Maudie), Eric Pohlmann (President), Michael Goodliffe (Commander), Wolfe Morris (Algeroccan Major), Michael Ripper (Ticket Collector), Patrick Holt (First Lieutenant), Charles Lloyd Pack (El Diabolo)

The Ugly Duckling (1959)
Credits: Director: Lance Comfort; Producers: Michael Carreras, Tommy Lyndon-Haynes; Screenplay: Sid Colin, Jack Davies; Production Company: Hammer Film Productions; Distributor: Columbia Pictures

Cast: Bernard Bresslaw (Henry Jekyll/Teddy Hyde), Jon Pertwee (Victor Jekyll), Richard Wattis (Barclay), David Lodge (Peewee), Michael Ripper (Fish), Harold

Goodwin (Benny), Michael Ward (Pasco), John Harvey (Barnes), Jess Conrad (Bimbo), Cyril Chamberlain (Police Sergeant), Roger Avon (Reporter)

The Man Who Could Cheat Death (1959)
Credits: Director: Terence Fisher; Producer: Michael Carreras; Screenplay: Jimmy Sangster; Production Company: Hammer Film Productions; Distributor: Paramount Pictues

Cast: Anton Diffring (Dr. Georges Bonner), Hazel Court (Janine Dubois), Christopher Lee (Dr. Pierre Gerrard), Arnold Marle (Dr. Ludwig Weiss), Francis de Wolff (Legris), Denis Shaw (Tavern Customer), Charles Lloyd Pack (Man), Lockwood West (First Doctor), Ronald Adam (Second Doctor), Michael Ripper (Morgue Attendant)

The Mummy (1959)
Credits: Director: Terence Fisher; Producer: Michael Carreras; Screenplay: Jimmy Sangster; Production Company: Hammer Film Productions; Distributor: Universal International

Cast: Peter Cushing (John Banning), Christopher Lee (The Mummy/Kharis), Yvonne Furneaux (Isobel/Ananka), Eddie Byrne (Inspector Murooney), Felix Aylmer (Stephen Banning), Raymond Huntley (Joseph Whemple), George Pastell (Mehemet Bey), Michael Ripper (Poacher), George Woodbridge (Police Constable), Harold Goodwin (Pat), Denis Shaw (Mike), Gerald Lawson (Irish Customer), Willoughby Gray (Dr. Reilly)

Bobbikins (1959)
Credits: Director: Robert Day; Producers: Oscar Brodney, Bob McNaught; Screenplay: Oscar Brodney; Production Company: 20th Century-Fox; Distributor: 20th Century-Fox

Cast: Max Bygraves (Benjamin Barnaby), Shirley Jones (Betty Barnaby), Billie Whitelaw (Lydia), Barbara Shelley (Valerie), Charles Tingwell (Luke), Lionel Jeffries (Gregory Mason), Rupurt Davies (Jock Fleming), David Lodge (Hargreave), Charles Lloyd Pack (Stebbins), Michael Ripper (Naval Petty Officer), Ronald Fraser (Sailor Joe)

Sink the Bismarck (1960)
Credits: Director: Lewis Gilbert; Producer: John Brabourne; Screenplay: Edmund H. North; Production Company: 20th Century-Fox; Distributor: 20th Century-Fox

Cast: Kenneth More (Captain Jonathan Shephard), Carl Mohner (Captain Lindemann), Laurence Naismith (First Sea Lord), Michael Hordern (Commander on King George), Maurice Denham (Richards), Michael Goodliffe (Captain Banister), Jack Watling (Signals Officer), Ernest Clark (Captain on Suffolk), Michael Ripper, Michael Balfour

Jackpot (1960)
Credits: Director: Montgomery Tully; Producer: Maurice J. Wilson; Screenplay: Maurice J. Wilson, Montgomery Tully; Production Company: Eternal; Distributor: Grand National

Cast: William Hartnell (Frawley), Betty McDowell (Kay Stock), Eddie Byrne (Sam Hare), Michael Ripper (Lenny Lane)

The Pure Hell of St. Trinian's (1960)
Credits: Director: Frank Launder; Producer: Sidney Gilliat; Screenplay: Frank Launder, Sidney Gilliat, Val Valentine; Production Company: British Lion; Distributor: British Lion

Cast: Cecil Parker (Canford), Joyce Grenfell (Ruby Gates), George Cole (Flash Harry), Thorley Walters (Butters), Eric Barker (Culpepper Brown), Irene Handl (Miss Harker Parker), Sidney James (Alphonse O'Reilly), Dennis Price (Gore Blackwood), Raymond Huntley (Judge), Liz Fraser (Miss Partridge), Cyril Chamberlain (Army Captain), George Benson (Defense Counsel), Michael Ripper (Liftman), John Le Mesurier (Minister)

Dead Lucky (1960)
Credits: Director: Montgomery Tully; Producers: Ralph Bond, Robert Dunbar; Screenplay: Sidney Nelson, Maurice Harrison; Production Company: ACT Films; Distributor: British Lion

Cast: Vincent Ball (Mike Billings), Betty McDowell (Jenny Drew), John Le Mesurier (Inspector Corcoran), Michael Ripper (Percy Simpson), Sam Kydd (Harry Winston)

Macbeth (1960)
Credits: Director: George Schaefer; Producer: Sidney Kaufman, Phil C. Samuel; Based on the Story by: William Shakespeare; Production Company: Grand Prize Films; Distributor: Prominent

Cast: Maurice Evans (Macbeth), Judith Anderson (Lady Macbeth), Michael Hordern (Banquo), Ian Bannen (Macduff), Felix Aylmer (Doctor), Megs Jenkins

(Gentlewoman), Jeremy Brett (Malcolm), Barry Warren (Donalbain), George Rose (Porter), Michael Ripper (First Murderer), Douglas Wilmer (Second Murderer)

Circle of Deception (1960)
Credits: Director: Jack Lee; Producer: Tom Monohan; Screenplay: Nigel Balchin, Robert Musel; Production Company: 20th Century-Fox; Distributor: 20th Century-Fox

Cast: Suzy Parker (Lucy Brown), Bradford Dillman (Paul Raine), Harry Andrews (Captain Rawson), Robert Stephens (Captain Stein), Charles Lloyd Pack (Ayres), Ronald Allen (Abelson), Duncan Lamont (Ballard), Michael Ripper (Chauvel), Frank Forsyth, Walter Gotell

Not a Hope in Hell (1960)
Credits: Director: Maclean Rogers; Producer: Roger Proudluck; Screenplay: Raymond Drews; Production Company: Parkside; Distributor: Archway

Cast: Richard Murcoch (Bertie), Sandra Dorne (Diana Melton), Jon Pertwee (Dan), Judith Furze (Miss Applejohn), Tim Turner (Cy Hallam), Claude Hulbert (Salter), Michael Ripper (Sid)

Brides of Dracula (1960)
Credits: Director: Terence Fisher; Producer: Anthony Hinds; Screenplay: Jimmy Sangster, Peter Bryan, Edward Percy; Production Company: Hammer Film Productions; Distributor: Universal International

Cast: Peter Cushing (Doctor Van Helsing), Martita Hunt (Baroness Meinster), Yvonne Monlaur (Marianne), Freda Jackson (Greta), David Peel (Baron Meinster), Miles Malleson (Dr. Tobler), Henry Oscar (Herr Lang), Mona Washbourne (Frau Lang), Fred Johnson (Cure), Michael Ripper (Coachman), Norman Pierce (Landlord), Michael Mulcaster (Latour)

The Curse of the Werewolf (1960)
Credits: Director: Terence Fisher; Producer: Anthony Hinds; Screenplay: John Elder; Production Company: Hammer Film Productions; Distributor: Universal International

Cast: Clifford Evans (Alfredo), Oliver Reed (Leon), Yvonne Romain (Servant Girl), Richard Wordsworth (The Beggar), Warren Mitchell (Pepe Valiente), George Woodbridge (Dominique), Michael Ripper (Old Soak), Ewen Solon (Don Fernando), Peter Sallis (Don Enrique)

Petticoat Pirates (1961)
Credits: Director: David Macdonald; Producer: Gordon L.T. Scott; Screenplay: Lew Schwartz, Charlie Drake; Production Company: Associated British Picture; Distributor: Warner Bros.

Cast: Charlie Drake (Charlie), Anne Heywood (Anne Stephens), Cecil Parker (Captain), Maxine Audley (Superintendent), Thorley Walters (Jerome Robertson), Victor Maddern (Nixon), Michael Ripper (Tug)

A Matter of Who (1961)
Credits: Director: Don Chaffey; Producers: Walter Shenson, Milton Holmes; Screenplay: Milton Holmes, Patricia Lee; Production Company: Foray; Distributor: M-G-M

Cast: Terry-Thomas (Archibald Bannister), Richard Briers (Jamieson), Honor Blackman (Sister Bryan), Carol White (Beryl), Martin Benson (Rahman), Geoffrey Keen (Foster), Michael Ripper (Skipper)

The Pirates of Blood River (1962)
Credits: Director: John Gilling; Producer: Anthony Hinds; Screenplay: John Hunter, John Gilling; Production Company: Hammer Film Productions; Distributor: Columbia Pictures

Cast: Kerwin Mathews (Jonathon Standing), Glenn Corbett (Henry), Christopher Lee (Captain La Roche), Marla Landi (Bess), Oliver Reed (Brocaire), Andrew Keir (Jason Standing), Peter Arne (Hench), Michael Ripper (Mac), David Lodge (Smith), Dennis Waterman (Timothy Blackthorne), Michael Mulcaster (William Martin), Denis Shaw (Silver)

Captain Clegg (1962)
Credits: Director: Peter Graham Scott; Producer: John Temple-Smith; Screenplay: John Elder, Barbara S. Harper; Production Company: Hammer Film Productions; Distributor: Universal International

Cast: Peter Cushing (Captain Clegg/Dr. Blyss), Yvonne Romain (Imogene), Patrick Allen (Captain Collier), Oliver Reed (Harry Crabtree), Michael Ripper (Jeremiah Mipps), Martin Benson (Rash), David Lodge (Bosun), Derek Francis (Squire), Sydney Bromley (Tom Ketch), Kate O'Mara (Girl in Inn)

The Phantom of the Opera (1962)
Credits: Director: Terence Fisher; Producer: Anthony Hinds; Screenplay: John Elder; Production Company: Hammer Film Productions; Distributor: Universal International

Cast: Herbert Lom (The Phantom/Professor Petrie), Heather Sears (Christine), Edward De Souza (Harry), Thorley Walters (Lattimer), Michael Gough (Ambrose), Harold Goodwin (Bill), Marne Maitland (Xavier), Miriam Karlin (Charwoman), Patrick Troughton (Ratcatcher), John Harvey (Sergeant Vickers), Michael Ripper (First Cabby), Miles Malleson (Second Cabby)

The Amorous Prawn (1962)
Credits: Director: Anthony Kimmins; Producer: Leslie Gilliat; Screenplay: Anthony Kimmins, Nicholas Phipps; Production Company: Covent Garden; Distributor: British Lion

Cast: Joan Greenwood (Lady Fitzadam), Cecil Parker (General Fitzadam), Ian Carmichael (Sidney Green), Robert Beatty (Larry Hoffman), Dennis Price (Prawn), Liz Fraser (Suzie Tidmarsh), Derek Nimmo (Willie Maltravers), Finlay Currie (Lochaye), Geoffrey Bayldon (Operator), Michael Ripper (Angus)

The Punch and Judy Man (1962)
Credits: Director: Jeremy Summers; Producer: Gordon L.T. Scott; Screenplay: Philip Oakes, Tony Hancock; Production Company: Macconkey; Distributor: Warner Bros.

Cast: Tony Hancock (Wally), Sylvia Syms (Delia), Ronald Fraser (Mayor), Barbara Murray (Lady Jane), John Le Mesurier (Sandman), Norman Bird (Committee Man), Peter Vaughan (Committee Man), Eddie Byrne (Ice Cream Man), Michael Ripper (Waiter)

Out of the Fog (1962)
Credits: Director: Montgomery Tully; Producer: Maurice J. Wilson; Screenplay: Montgomery Tully; Production Company: Eternal; Distributor: Grand National

Cast: David Summer (George Mallon), Susan Travers (June Lock), James Hayter (Daniels), Jack Watson (Sergeant Tracey), George Woodbridge (Chopper), Michael Ripper (Tich)

A Prize of Arms (1962)
Credits: Director: Cliff Owen; Producer: George Maynard; Screenplay: Paul Ryder; Production Company: Bryanston; Distributor: British Lion

Cast: Stanley Baker (Turpin), Tom Bell (Fenner), Tom Adams (Glenn), Rodney Bewes (Private Maynard), Stephen Lewis (Bates), Fulton Mackay (Henderson), Patrick Magee (Hicks), Michael Ripper (Freeman)

Two Left Feet (1962)
Credits: Director: Roy Baker; Producer: Leslie Gilliat; Screenplay: Roy Baker, John Hopkins; Production Company: British Lion; Distributor: British Lion

Cast: Michael Crawford (Alan Crabbe), Nyree Dawn Porter (Eileen), David Hemmings (Brian), David Lodge (Bill), Bernard Lee (Mr. Crabbe), Cyril Chamberlain (Miles), Neil McCarthy (Ted), Michael Ripper (Uncle Reg)

The Prince and the Pauper (1962)
Credits: Director: Don Chaffey; Producer: Hugh Attwooll; Screenplay: Jack Whittingham; Production Company: Walt Disney; Distributor: Walt Disney

Cast: Guy Williams (Miles Hendon), Laurence Naismith (Hertford), Donald Houston (John Canty), Sean Scully (Edward/Tom), Niall MacGinnis (Father Andrew), Geoffrey Keen (Yokel), Jane Asher (Lady Jane Grey), Peter Butterworth (Will), Reginald Beckwith (Landlord), Michael Ripper, Norman Mitchell

What a Crazy World (1963)
Credits: Director: Michael Carreras; Producer: Michael Carreras; Screenplay: Alan Klein, Michael Carreras; Production Company: Capricorn, Associated British Picture; Distributor: Warner Bros.

Cast: Joe Brown (Alf Hitchens), Susan Maughan (Marilyn), Marty Wilde (Herbie Shadbolt), Harry H. Corbett (Sam Hitchens), Avis Bunnage (Mary Hitchens), Michael Ripper (Common Man), Larry Dann (Chas), Bill Fraser (Milligan), Michael Robbins

The Scarlet Blade (1963)
Credits: Director: John Gilling; Producer: Anthony Nelson-Keys; Screenplay: John Gilling; Production Company: Hammer Film Productions; Distributor: Columbia Pictures

Cast: Lionel Jeffries (Colonel Judd), Oliver Reed (Captain Sylvester), June Thorburn (Clare Judd), Duncan Lamont (Major Bell), Suzan Farmer (Constance), Michael Ripper (Pablo), John Harvey (Grey), George Woodbridge (Town Crier)

Devil-Ship Pirates (1964)
Credits: Director: Don Sharp; Producer: Anthony Nelson-Keys; Screenplay: Jimmy Sangster; Production Company: Hammer Film Productions; Distributor: Columbia Pictures

Cast: Christopher Lee (Captain Robeles), Andrew Keir (Tom), John Cairney (Harry), Duncan Lamont (The Bosun), Michael Ripper (Pepe), Ernest Clark (Sir Basil), Barry Warren (Manuel), Suzan Farmer (Angela), Natasha Pyne (Jane), Johnny Briggs (Pablo)

The Curse of the Mummy's Tomb (1964)
Credits: Director: Michael Carreras; Producer: Michael Carreras; Screenplay: Henry Younger; Production Company: Hammer Film Productions; Distributor: Columbia Pictures

Cast: Terence Morgan (Adam Beauchamp), Ronald Howard (John Bray), Fred Clark (Alexander King), Jeanne Roland (Annette Dubois), George Pastell (Hashmi Bey), Michael Ripper (Achmed), Harold Goodwin (Fred), Marianne Stone (Landlady)

Every Day's a Holiday (1964)
Credits: Director: James Hill; Producer: Ronald J. Kahn; Screenplay: Anthony Marriott, Jeri Matos, James Hill; Production Company: Fitzroy-Maycroft; Distributor: Grand National

Cast: John Leyton (Gerry Pullman), Ron Moody (Bastinado), Liz Fraser (Miss Slightly), Nicholas Parsons (Julian Goddard), Michael Ripper (Mr. Pullman), Richard O'Sullivan (Jimmy), Peter Gilmore (Kenneth), Charles Lloyd Pack (Mr. Close)

Secret of Blood Island (1965)
Credits: Director: Quentin Lawrence; Producer: Anthony Nelson-Keys; Screenplay: John Gilling; Production Company: Hammer Film Productions; Distributor: Universal International

Cast: Jack Hedley (Sergeant Crews), Barbara Shelley (Elaine), Patrick Wymark (Jocomo), Charles Tingwell (Major Dryden), Bill Owen (Bludgin), Lee Montague (Levy), Edwin Richfield (O'Reilly), Michael Ripper (Japanese Driver), Glyn Houston (Berry)

The Reptile (1965)
Credits: Director: John Gilling; Producer: Anthony Nelson-Keys; Screenplay: John Elder; Production Company: Hammer Film Productions; Distributor: 20th Century-Fox

Cast: Noel Willman (Dr. Franklyn), Jennifer Daniel (Valerie), Ray Barrett (Harry), Jacqueline Pearce (Anna), Michael Ripper (Tom Bailey), John Laurie

(Mad Peter), Marne Maitland (Malay), Charles Lloyd Pack (Vicar), George Woodbridge (Old Garnsey)

The Plague of the Zombies (1965)
Credits: Director: John Gilling; Producer: Anthony Nelson-Keys; Screenplay: Peter Bryan; Production Company: Hammer Film Productions; Distributor: 20th Century-Fox

Andre Morell (Sir James Forbes), Diane Clare (Sylvia), Brook Williams (Dr. Peter Tompson), Jacqueline Pearce (Alice), John Carson (Clive Hamilton), Michael Ripper (Sergeant Swift), Marcus Hammond (Martinus), Ben Aris (John Martinus)

The Spy Who Came in from the Cold (1965)
Credits: Director: Martin Ritt; Producer: Martin Ritt; Screenplay: Paul Dehn, Guy Trosper; Production Company: Salem; Distributor: Paramount Pictures

Cast: Richard Burton (Alec Leamas), Claire Bloom (Nan Perry), Rupert Davies (Smiley), Cyril Cusack (Control), Michael Hordern (Ashe), Robert Hardy (Carlton), Bernard Lee (Patmore), Esmond Knight (Old Judge), Niall MacGinnis (German Checkpoint Guard), Michael Ripper (Lofthouse), Warren Mitchell (Mr. Zanfrello)

Where the Bullets Fly (1966)
Credits: Director: John Gilling; Producer: James Ward; Screenplay: Michael Pittock; Production Company: Puck; Distributor: Golden Era Film

Cast: Tom Adams (Charles Vine), Dawn Addams (Felicity Moonlight), Sidney James (Mortuary Attendant), Wilfrid Brambell (Train Guard), Michael Ripper (Angel), Ronald Leigh-Hunt (Thrusby), Marcus Hammond (O'Neil), Michael Ward (Michael), Bryan Mosley (Connolly), Suzan Farmer (Caron), James Ellis (Fotheringham), Michael Balfour (Bandleader)

The Mummy's Shroud (1966)
Credits: Director: John Gilling; Producer: Anthony Nelson-Keys; Screenplay: John Gilling; Production Company: Hammer Film Productions; Distributor: 20th Century-Fox

Cast: Andre Morell (Sir Basil Walden), John Phillips (Stanley Preston), David Buck (Paul Preston), Elizabeth Sellars (Barbara Preston), Michael Ripper (Longbarrow), Roger Delgado (Hasmid), Catherine Lacey (Haiti), Dickie Owen (Prem), Eddie Powell (The Mummy)

The Great St. Trinian's Train Robbery (1966)
Credits: Directors: Frank Launder, Sidney Gilliat; Producers: Frank Launder, Sidney Gilliat; Screenplay: Frank Launder, Ivor Herbert; Production Company: Braywild; Distributor: British Lion

Cast: Frankie Howard (Alphonse Askett), Reg Varney (Gilbert), Cyril Chamberlain (Maxie), Arthur Mullard (Big Jim), Raymond Huntley (The Minister), Richard Wattis (Manton Bassett), Peter Gilmore (Butters), Eric Barker (Culpepper Brown), George Benson (Gore Blackwood), Michael Ripper (Liftman), Dora Bryan (Amber Spottiswood), Carole Ann Ford (Albertine), George Cole (Flash Harry), Norman Mitchell (The Toastmaster), Aubrey Morris (Hutch), Terry Scott

Torture Garden (1967)
Credits: Director: Freddie Francis; Producer: Max J. Rosenberg, Milton Subotsky; Screenplay: Robert Bloch; Production Company: Amicus; Distributor: Columbia Pictures

Cast: Jack Palance (Ronald Wyatt), Burgess Meredith (Dr. Diabolo), Peter Cushing (Lancelot Canning), Barbara Ewing (Dorothy Endicott), Michael Bryant (Colin Williams), Maurice Denham (Colin's Uncle), John Standing (Leo Winston), Michael Ripper (Gordon Roberts), Catherine Finn (Nurse Parker), Ursula Howells (Miss Chambers), Niall MacGinnis (Doctor)

The Deadly Bees (1967)
Credits: Director: Freddie Francis; Producers: Max J. Rosenberg, Milton Subotsky; Screenplay: Robert Block, Anthony Marriott; Production Company: Amicus; Distributor: Paramount Pictures

Cast: Suzanna Leigh (Vicki Robbins), Frank Finlay (Manfred), Guy Doleman (Hargrove), Catherine Finn (Mrs. Hargrove), John Harvey (Thompson), Michael Ripper (David Hawkins), James Cossins (Coroner), Frank Forsyth (Doctor), Katy Wild (Doris Hawkins), Michael Gwynn (Dr. Lang)

Inspector Clouseau (1968)
Credits: Director: Bud Yorkin; Producer: Lewis Rachmil; Screenplay: Frank Waldman; Production Company: Mirisch; Distributor: United Artists

Cast: Alan Arkin (Inspector James Clouseau), Frank Finlay (Superintendent Weaver), Patrick Cargill (Sir Charles Braithwaite), Beryl Reid (Mrs. Weaver), Barry Foster (Addison Steele), Michael Ripper (Frey), Anthony Ainley (Bomber LeBec), George Pravda (Wulf), Eric Pohlmann (Bergesch), Geoffrey Bayldon (Gutch), Robert Russell (Stockton)

The Lost Continent (1968)
Credits: Director: Michael Carreras; Producer: Michael Carreras; Screenplay: Michael Nash; Production Company: Hammer Film Productions; Distributor: 20th Century-Fox

Cast: Eric Porter (Captain Lansen), Suzanna Leigh (Unity), Nigel Stock (Dr. Webster), Neil McCallum (1st Officer Hemmings), Jimmy Hanley (Pat), James Cossins (Chief), Victor Maddern (Mate), Norman Eshley (Jonathan), Michael Ripper (Sea Lawyer), Donald Sumpter (Sparks), Eddie Powell (Inquisitor)

Dracula Has Risen from the Grave (1968)
Credits: Director: Freddie Francis; Producer: Aida Young; Screenplay: John Elder; Production Company: Hammer Film Productions; Distributor: Warner Bros.

Cast: Christopher Lee (Dracula), Rupert Davies (Monsignor), Veronica Carlson (Maria), Barbara Ewing (Zena), Barry Andrews (Paul), Ewan Hooper (Priest), Michael Ripper (Max), George A. Cooper (Landlord)

Mumsy, Nanny, Sonny, and Girly (1969)
Credits: Director: Freddie Francis; Producer: Ronald J. Kahn; Screenplay: Brian Comport; Production Company: Brigitte-Fitzroy-Francis; Distributor: Cinerama

Cast: Michael Bryant (New Friend), Ursula Howells (Mumsy), Pat Heywood (Nanny), Howard Trevor (Sonny), Vanessa Howard (Girly), Robert Swann (Soldier), Imogen Hassall (Girl Friend), Michael Ripper (Zoo Attendant)

Moon Zero Two (1969)
Credits: Director: Roy Ward Baker; Producer: Michael Carreras; Screenplay: Michael Carreras; Production Company: Hammer Film Productions; Distributor: Warner Bros.

Cast: James Olson (Kemp), Catherine Von Schell (Clem), Warren Mitchell (Hubbard), Adrienne Corri (Liz), Bernard Bresslaw (Harry), Neil McCallum (Space Captain), Michael Ripper (Card Player), Sam Kydd (Barman)

Taste the Blood of Dracula (1969)
Credits: Director: Peter Sasdy; Producer: Aida Young; Screenplay: John Elder; Production Company: Hammer Film Productions; Distributor: Warner Bros.

Cast: Christopher Lee (Dracula), Geoffrey Keen (William Hargood), Gwen Watford (Martha Hargood), Peter Sallis (Samuel Paxton), Anthony Corlan (Paul Paxton), Isla Blair (Lucy Paxton), John Carson (Jonathan Secker), Martin Jarvis (Jeremy Secker), Ralph Bates (Lord Courtley), Roy Kinnear (Welller), Michael Ripper (Cobb)

Scars of Dracula (1970)
Credits: Director: Roy Ward Baker; Producer: Aida Young; Screenplay: John Elder; Production Company: Hammer Film Productions; Distributor: EMI

Cast: Christopher Lee (Dracula), Dennis Waterman (Simon), Jenny Hanley (Sarah), Christopher Matthews (Paul), Patrick Troughton (Klove), Michael Gwynn (Priest), Michael Ripper (Landlord), Bob Todd (Burgomaster), Toke Townley (Elderly Wagonner)

That's Your Funeral (1971)
Credits: Director: John Robins; Producer: Michael Carreras; Screenplay: Peter Lewis; Production Company: Hammer Film Productions; Distributor: Rank

Cast: Bill Fraser (Basil Bulstrode), Raymond Huntley (Emanuel Holroyd), David Battley (Percy), Dennis Price (Mr. Soul), Sue Lloyd (Miss Peach), Richard Wattis (Simmonds), Roy Kinnear (Mr. Purvis), Eric Barker (Pusher), Michael Ripper (Arthur), Frank Thornton (Town Clerk), Peter Copley (Director), Bob Todd, Michael Robbins

The Creeping Flesh (1972)
Credits: Director: Freddie Francis; Producer: Michael Redbourn; Screenplay: Peter Spenceley, Jonathan Rumbold; Production Company: Tigon; Distributor: Columbia Pictures

Cast: Christopher Lee (Dr. James Hildern), Peter Cushing (Professor Emmanuel Hildern), Lorna Heilbron (Penelope Hildern), George Benson (Waterloo), Kenneth J. Warren (Lenny), Duncan Lamont (Inspector), Harry Locke (Barman), Michael Ripper (Carter), Catherine Finn (Emily), David Bailie (Young Doctor), Marianne Stone (Assistant)

No Sex Please, We're British (1973)
Credits: Director: Cliff Owen; Producer: John R. Sloan; Screenplay: Anthony Marriott, Johnnie Mortimer, Brian Cooke; Production Company: B.H.P. Films; Distributor: Columbia Pictures

Cast: Ronnie Corbett (Brian Runnicles), Beryl Reid (Bertha Hunter), Arthur Lowe (Mr. Bromley), Ian Ogilvy (David Hunter), Susan Penhaligon (Penny

Hunter), Deryck Guyler (Park Keeper), Valerie Leon (Susan), Michael Robbins (Car Driver), Frank Thornton (Glass Shop Manager), Michael Ripper (Traffic Warden), Sydney Bromley (Rag, Bone Man), Stephen Greif (Niko), Brian Wilde (Policeman), Robin Askwith (Baker's Delivery Man)

Legend of the Werewolf (1974)
Credits: Director: Freddie Francis; Producer: Kevin Francis; Screenplay: John Elder; Production Company: Tyburn; Distributor: Rank

Cast: Peter Cushing (Professor Paul Cataflanque), Ron Moody (Zookeeper), Hugh Griffith (Maestro Pamponi), Roy Castle (Photographer), David Rintoul (Etoile), Marjorie Yates (Madame Tellier), Norman Mitchell (Tiny), David Bailie (Boulon), Michael Ripper (Sewerman), Patrick Holt (Dignitary), John Harvey (Prefect of Police)

The Prince and the Pauper (1977) (U.S. title: **Crossed Swords**)
Credits: Director: Richard Fleischer; Producer: Pierre Spengler; Screenplay: George Macdonald Fraser; Production Company: Alexander and Ilya Salkind; Distributor: Warner Bros.

Cast: Oliver Reed (Miles Hendon), Raquel Welch (Lady Edith), Mark Lester (Edward/Tom), Ernest Borgnine (John Canty), George C. Scott (Ruffian), Charlton Heston (Henry VIII), Rex Harrison (The Duke of Norfolk), David Hemmings (Hugh Hendon), Harry Andrews (Hertford), Lalla Ward (Princess Elizabeth), Sybil Danning (Mother Canty), Graham Stark (Jester), Preston Lockwood (Father Andrew), Don Henderson (Burly Ruffian), Sydney Bromley (Peasant), Ruth Madoc (Moll), Dudley Sutton (Hodge), Anthony Sharp (Dr. Buttes), Peter Cellier (Mean Man), Michael Ripper (Edith's Servant), Norman Mitchell

Sammy's Super T-Shirt (1978)
Credits: Director: Jeremy Summers; Producer: Frank Godwin; Screenplay: Frank Godwin; Production Company: Monument; Distributor: Children's Film Foundation

Cast: Reggie Winch (Sammy Smith), Richard Vernon (Beckett), Julian Holloway (Trotter), Patsy Rowlands (Mum), Michael Ripper (Gateman), Marianne Stone (Neighbor)

Danger on Dartmoor (1980)
Credits: Director: David Eady; Producer: Mike Gorell-Barnes; Screenplay: Dudley Leslie; Production Company: Eady-Barnes; Distributor: Children's Film Foundation

Cast: Marcus Evans (Robin Chudleigh), Simon Henderson (Jonathan Chudleigh), Barry Foster (Green), Patricia Hayes (Mrs. Green), Sam Kydd, Michael Ripper

No Surrender (1985)
Credits: Director: Peter Smith; Producer: Mamoun Hassan; Screenplay: Alan Bleasdale; Production Company: Film Four; Distributor: Palace Pictures

Cast: Michael Angelis (Mike), Avis Bunnage (Martha), James Ellis (Paddy), Bernard Hill (Bernard), Ray McAnally (Billy), Joanne Whalley (Cheryl), J.G. Devlin (George), Vince Earl (Frank), Ken Jones (Ron), Michael Ripper (Tony Bonaparte)

Revenge of Billy the Kid (1991)
Credits: Director: Jim Groom; Producer: Tim Dennison; Screenplay: Tim Dennison, Jim Groom, Richard Matthews; Production Company: Montage; Distributor: Powerhouse Pictures

Cast: Michael Balfour (Gyles MacDonald), Norman Mitchell (Mr. Allott), Michael Ripper (Old Fisherman), Samantha Perkins, Jackie D. Broad, Trevor Peake

About the Author

Derek was born and lives in Yorkshire, England.

He is a professional actor and British Equity Member and started his acting career at the age of 14 appearing in the film *The Gun.*

He later went on to study drama at The North Cheshire Theatre School in Manchester, England.

Theatrical work includes *Trummi Kaput* (Tour Of Germany) and touring productions in England of *Sweeney Todd*, *A Midsummer Night's Dream* (playing Bottom), *Oliver* (playing Fagin) and *A Christmas Carol* (playing Scrooge).

Derek Pykett (Photograph by Sandy Collis)

Derek has also appeared in several Charity Variety Shows, which include portraying William Shakespeare in a Variety Show at the Sadler's Wells Theatre in London.

On English Television he appeared in *Coasting* (Granada TV), *Emmerdale* (Yorkshire TV) and more recently played a Squatter in *Peak Practice* for Central TV in England.

Films include *Stanley's Dragon*, *Criminal* and *The Princess Bride* directed by Rob Reiner.

This is Derek's first biography.

John Stell, the author of *Psychos! Sickos! and Sequels*: *Horror Films from the 1980s* from Midnight Marquee Press, is a contributor to *Midnight Marquee* and *Monsters from the Vault*.

If you enjoyed this book
visit our website
at www.midmar.com
or call for a free catalog
410-665-1198
Midnight Marquee Press, Inc.
9721 Britinay Lane
Baltimore, MD 21234

9 781887 664271